YOU

The Last Best Hope to Restore Our Nation

To my Family—

Julie—the love of my life and best friend

Tyler, Keeley, Betsy—my treasures in this life. No man could be more blessed.

About The Author

Bill is a retired Intelligence Officer who served a 30-year career in the United States Marine Corps. He enlisted as a private in 1975, and after four years of active service, he left the Marine Corps as a sergeant to pursue studies at Eastern Montana College. While there, he joined the Platoon Leaders Class, and, upon graduation from college in December 1985, he was commissioned as a second lieutenant and returned to active duty in the Marine Corps. He served on active duty until 2011 when he retired as a Colonel. Throughout his career in the Marine Corps, he served in both command and staff positions around the world.

During Operation IRAQI FREEDOM, he served as the Iraq All Source Team Chief in the Joint Intelligence Center for USCENTCOM in Qatar. He then returned to Tampa for a short period before he deployed to Baghdad in July 2003, to establish the National Intelligence Center.

Bill assumed command of 3rd Radio Battalion, Kaneohe Bay, Hawaii, in July 2004, and deployed to Al Anbar Province, Iraq, in support of II Marine Expeditionary Force from June

2005 through February 2006. In July 2009, he assumed command of Marine Corps Intelligence Schools, Dam Neck, Virginia, and served there until his retirement. Bill resides in Bozeman, Montana, with the love of his life and wife of twenty-nine years, Julie. They have three grown children.

Acknowledgements

Passion alone does not get a book written or published. After a life of enjoying the written word, I was unaware of how unprepared I was to attempt to write a book myself. The initial drafts of the chapters of this book and the final product you are about to read have little in common. There are a few people I'd like to thank for the instrumental roles they played in bringing this little venture to completion.

First of all, none of this would have been possible if it were not for the unending encouragement and patient support of my best friend and wife, Julie. She would—after a long-day's work—edit and critique the chapters I had ground out during the day until she could no longer keep her eyes open.

I next handed it off to Patricia McAllister, my mother-in-law, who took on the second-phase editing challenge with passion and diplomacy. It was pure joy; we had many long talks and shared perspectives and positive suggestions for improvement. It was truly a labor of love; she had to translate my colloquialisms into the English language without losing my intent.

When I was finally comfortable enough to turn this project over to a professional, a good friend and fellow Marine gave me the name of a Marine he had served with. I figured that at least she would extend some professional courtesy and not laugh at me. What she did with the rough I gave her was truly amazing. I'm not sure I will ever attempt to write another book, but if I do, I know who I want to edit it. Nancy Broding (www.npbediting.com) took an idea and made it a reality—from finish-editing to publishing. You would not be reading this but for her professionalism and expertise.

I would also like to thank Bill Federer of American Minute and an author of over 20 books. Bill inspired me to try and write a book and then took the time to guide me through the process. He also introduced me to Dustin Myers of Longitude design who created the book cover. Many thanks for the collective patience and professionalism you have all shown me; I really had no idea what it took to write and publish a book.

Most of all, I thank God. I have no idea where life would have taken me without His mercy and grace in my life.

Table of Contents

Preface

It is nearly impossible to keep up with the changes that are occurring in our nation. Daily those waves of change roll across our nation with increasing frequency and intensity. The world stage is becoming progressively more unstable with economic uncertainty and nations constantly in conflict or war. To the average individual it can seem overwhelming, but you are not the average individual. You are an American endowed with certain inalienable rights from your Creator. The power to restore our nation does not abide in a president, legislature, or the judicial system. The only one who can shore up the shifting sands is *you*—empowered by the universal strengths of truth, justice and love. Evil can only prosper if good men and women do nothing.

The America I Grew Up In

I grew up in a carefree time that was certainly less confusing than today. I learned many of the lessons of life from two full-time parents who modeled both love and discipline. Fathers, and sometimes mothers, worked and provided for their families. If you wanted something, you learned to work for it. If your parents could not afford something, you simply did not have it. There was a stigma associated with receiving food stamps and welfare. Unemployment was a safety net most did not want to use. We had dinner as a family and then were allowed to play until the streetlights came on. We played outside, spring, summer, fall, and winter, with minimal adult supervision manifested only when actions of wayward children warranted intervention from grown-ups, whether involving their own children or someone else's children. These adults acted in good faith with the best interests of the children at heart—and did so without fear of consequences from other parents. At 10 years old I could walk to the store and purchase .22 shells for my single shot rifle and walk out of town and hunt small game.

We walked to and from school without our parents worrying if we were going to be abducted. We went to school to learn how to read, write, and do arithmetic. Teachers were the authority inside the classroom and on the school grounds. Bad behavior was not tolerated. It was years later when I learned that the "board of education" was not the wooden paddle hanging in the principal's office. If I got in trouble at school, I could guarantee I was going to be in more trouble at home. We were taught to respect our elders, respect the police, and anyone else in a position of authority.

If you were born with male anatomy you used a men's rest room. If you were born with female anatomy you used a women's rest room. You were not allowed to decide. We competed in school, we competed in sports, and we competed in life. We learned to earn self-esteem; it was not something that was given to you at the school. Trophies and ribbons were given to the top three finishers in academics and sports and the rest of us knew we would have to work harder if we wanted recognition.

I grew up in a time when nobody locked their homes or cars. Everyone was taught to respect other people's property and it was understood you did not enter without permission. As I got older, we would drive to school with loaded rifles or shotguns in our cars because we had been hunting before school or were going hunting after school. We would leave firearms in our unlocked cars, the thought never crossing our minds to bring a weapon into school.

The county sheriff and deputies were known as "peace officers" and they were just that. They did not spend their time trying to find someone who was breaking the law to ticket or throw into jail. They maintained the peace. Many times we could have been ticketed or even charged with some offense, but instead they sent us home with a verbal warning they were going to follow up with our parents.

Most families attended church on Sunday. It certainly did not necessarily mean that they believed in God, but society as a whole was exposed to the principles of morality and religion each week. We were ingrained with the thought that life was not without consequences and that there was an ultimate responsibility to God. Religion provided the unwritten law of accountability. People were still people, but at least there was shame attached to immoral or unethical behavior.

We were raised to believe in our country; most of our fathers had served in World War II. Every morning we said the Pledge of Allegiance to the United States flag. We stood rigidly at attention when the national anthem was played. We were proud to be Americans and knew we lived in the greatest country on earth. We were taught the evils of communism and the blessings of freedom. The thought never entered our minds to fear the government. It was there to help, not hinder—to advise, not control.

The America of Today

We have experienced decades of unrestrained government growth in size, regulation, and debt. We meddle in the affairs of the world. The government has become an organization that creates solutions looking for problems. These solutions come with high price tags and over-reaching legislation.

The America of today has become a nation of people who fear our government and have little hope for a better future. This did not happen overnight and will not be fixed overnight. We have been acting like absentee landlords who left our property to managers who had no concern for the well-being of the property and were only concerned with the wealth that could be accumulated. Our founders did not intend for our government to be a spectator sport. They believed "We the People" would control the government and not let the government control us. We have totally abdicated that control to lesser men who desire position, wealth, and power above all else.

These same men routinely ignore the "rule of law"—our United States Constitution—and package legislation under the guise of providing security and social justice.

Fear and social justice have become the two driving forces for fundamentally changing the nation. As a people we have traded freedom for a false sense of security. The extreme vocal voice of the minority seeks to re-engineer the culture of the majority through threat, intimidation, and political correctness. To sit back and remain silent while hoping your life will be unaffected is no longer an option if you are to continue to live in a free nation.

Communism is in vogue; patriots and people who choose to talk about the Constitution are labeled as extremists. The government places Christians, combat veterans, pro-life citizens, and those who speak with anti-globalist principles on domestic terror watch lists. Flag burners are celebrated, people sit for the national anthem, and children are not required to pledge allegiance to the flag. A recent article on *World Net Daily* reports that the most persecuted religious group is

Christians.[1] God has been kicked out of the public square, and soon Christianity will be labeled as "hate speech."

Today, marriage is a casual relationship that can be discarded for any reason without social stigma. Fathers, and sometimes mothers, can be absent, present, deadbeat, biological, step, or foster. The government is here to provide food, housing, education, and medical assistance. If you decide to spend your paycheck on big screen TV's, car loans, drugs, or alcohol, the government will ensure you have everything else including multiple cell phones, your favorite beverage, and chips.

Schools have moved past basic education to social engineering. Children in elementary school can now learn about their sexuality; in fact, they are introduced to alternative sexual behavior before they have any interest in sex. They learn that they can be homosexual, transgender, or gender flexible, and they can use any restroom they want.

Teachers are not allowed to discipline. Children who act up can be sedated; and everyone passes their grade and is promoted to the next. Parents defend bad behavior, and school

---

[1] Bob Unruh, "Christians 'Most Persecuted Religious Group'," *World Net Daily* 25 May 2015, http://www.wnd.com/2015/05/most-persecuted-religious-group-in-world-is/

administrators have to build a case to discipline bad behavior. Children now bring weapons into schools to kill fellow students, teachers, and principals. In sports, our youth are taught that everyone gets a trophy.

Private property is no longer private property; the government can tax and regulate your property. There are thousands of regulations designed to limit your use of your property. Respect for the property of others is an idea that is almost extinct.

"Peace Officers" have transitioned to "Law Enforcement Officers," with generation of revenue taking precedence over maintaining the peace. We now have over 80,000 SWAT raids each year. Many departments choose to use an axe when a scalpel would better serve the purpose. The average citizen lacks respect for the police and the law now that we have transitioned to a mentality of "guilty until proven innocent" or "how much is this going to cost me to go away."

Personal accountability and responsibility, morality, and religion were the cornerstones of what made our nation free and prosperous. What we see now is lack of accountability or responsibility in our elected officials, the complete erosion of morality, and a government assault on religion. The United

States is a country founded on Judeo-Christian principles that now plays host to many of the world's anti-Christian agendas.

External forces do not destroy great nations, but rather great nations are destroyed from within. The United States is following the same course that other nations followed and that eventually lead to their downfall.

This is a book about your responsibility to God and country and it is aimed at providing you with the tools to lead in home, schools, businesses, and government. You will not eliminate poverty or bring peace to the world, but you will be equipped to restore our nation. The following quote is taken from Bill Federer's *American Minute* on April 3, 2015. Edward Everett Hale, the grandnephew of Revolutionary hero Nathan Hale, who became Chaplain of the United States Senate in 1903, wrote, "*I am only one, but I am one. I cannot do everything, but I can do something. What I can do, I should do and, with the help of God, I will do.*"

Our nation will not be restored by politicians or political parties. It is not in their best interests to willingly give up power, influence, fame, or fortune to the people.

At the close of the Constitutional Convention in September 1787, Benjamin Franklin was asked by Mrs. Powel of Philadelphia, "*Well, Doctor, what have we got, a republic or a monarchy?*" Franklin replied, "*A republic, if you can keep it.*" It's up to you; only you can restore our nation.

The Most Powerful Government in the World

"America is like a healthy body and its resistance is threefold: its patriotism, its morality, and its spiritual life. If we can undermine these three areas, America will collapse from within."

—Josef Stalin

As we understand Russia under Stalin, it was a godless, totalitarian, communist state in which all power was centralized in the government, a nationalist society brought about by the extermination of millions of dissenters. Citizens had no rights guaranteed by the government—privileges, not rights, were only maintained by staying in favor with the government.

The United States stood in direct contrast to Russia. God was indeed the centerpiece of the lives of most citizens. God is mentioned four times in the Declaration of

Independence. The first two paragraphs decree that man's rights come from God, not government:

> *When in the Course of human events, it becomes necessary for one people to dissolve the political bands which have connected them with another, and to assume among the powers of the earth, the separate and equal station to which the Laws of Nature and of Nature's God entitle them, a decent respect to the opinions of mankind requires that they should declare the causes which impel them to the separation.*

> *We hold these truths to be self-evident, that all men are created equal, that they are endowed by their Creator with certain unalienable Rights, that among these are Life, Liberty and the pursuit of Happiness.— That to secure these rights, Governments are instituted among Men, deriving their just powers from the consent of the governed...*

Stalin understood the strength of America didn't come from the iron fist of the government but from a patriotic, moral, God-fearing people.

In Russia's case, morality was defined by the state. In the case of the United States, morality is defined first by God who gives us our rights, and then by the individuals who live by a moral code established not by man but by God.

> *No people will tamely surrender their Liberties, nor can any be easily subdued, when knowledge is diffused and Virtue is preserved. On the Contrary, when People are universally ignorant, and debauched in their Manners, they will sink under their own weight without the Aid of foreign Invaders.*
>
> —Samuel Adams

The United States today retains the largest prison population in the world at over two million. That is more than the combined total of all prison populations of other developed nations. According to the Government Accountability Office, 25 percent of those incarcerated in federal prisons are illegal aliens.

In the wake of the shooting death of Michael Brown in Ferguson, Missouri, we saw mobs burn and loot businesses for sport. Following the death of Freddie Gray in Baltimore, mobs vandalized and looted over 30 businesses, 144 vehicles and 15 buildings were incinerated, and 61 structural fires occurred, resulting in approximately $9 million in damages.

Various studies show that more than 90 percent of children and teens play video games, most of which contain violent content. A study from Drexel University reported that 50 percent of the university students surveyed reported that as minors they engaged in sexting—exchanging sexually explicit text messages with or without photographic images. We see teens inventing new disturbing games like "knockout," where they approach unsuspecting men, women and children and try to knock them out with a single punch—just for the fun of it.

The once entertaining *Leave it to Beaver, I Love Lucy,* and *My Three Sons* television programming has evolved into a no-holds-barred sexually explicit, linguistically vulgar, and morally disturbing bombardment of so-called "reality TV" shows. The Internet has become the largest purveyor of pornography the world has ever experienced, with over 78 million households in the U.S. with broadband connectivity.

Today, 50 percent of all children born in the U.S. are born out of wedlock. As a nation we average over one million abortions per year. The U.S. government provides over five hundred million tax dollars per year to Planned Parenthood, the largest abortion provider in the country. Recently-aired videos show how Planned Parenthood harvests organs from babies and then sells them like crop futures on the open market.

Pages could be filled illustrating how citizens have cast off any sort of moral restraint. This is certainly one thing we cannot blame on the government. Corrupt government does not cause moral decay; moral decay gives birth to corrupt government. Good government comes from a moral, virtuous people. The United States became a great nation because the people were a moral and religious people.

"Only a virtuous people are capable of freedom. As nations become corrupt and vicious, they have more need of masters."
—Benjamin Franklin

The following was taken from a letter John Adams wrote to the Officers of the First Brigade of the Third Division of the Militia of Massachusetts on October 11, 1798:

We have no government armed with power capable of contending with human passions unbridled by morality and religion. Avarice, ambition, revenge, or gallantry, would break the strongest cords of our Constitution as a whale goes through a net. Our Constitution was made only for a moral and religious people. It is wholly inadequate to the government of any other.

The founders wrote a Constitution to provide the most individual freedom the world had ever known, but that freedom was maintained by individual morality. They understood that man had to restrain his own actions if the country was going to remain free. They also recognized that individual morality stemmed from an unchanging moral code established by God and maintained by a religious people. God, not man, established the very basis for freedom and justice.

After studying history, our founding fathers understood that the morality of a nation originated in the individual and was not corporately established by government. History reveals the failure of both government-established religion and government-established morality. If man does not control his actions, then the government does; otherwise, society will collapse into anarchy. If the government controls you, you have tyranny; if you control yourself, you have liberty. If government legislates morality, then it can only do so by attempting to restrict the passions of man through law. Eventually, you end up with a totalitarian state with a strong central government that restricts the life, liberty, and pursuit of happiness for all.

The founders were focused on the smallest, most powerful government in the world: self-government. Self-government is simply a man's ability to rule himself, to exercise control over himself.

Both our founders and our adversaries put a lot of stock in morality and religion. The question is: If morality and religion are taken away, does patriotism survive on its own? Not according to George Washington. In his farewell address to Congress, he said it was vain for a man to claim patriotism who would subvert religion and morality:

> *Of all the dispositions and habits which lead to political prosperity, religion and morality are indispensable supports. In vain would that man claim the tribute of patriotism, who should labor to subvert these great pillars of*

human happiness, these firmest props of the duties of men and citizens. The mere politician, equally with the pious man, ought to respect and to cherish them. A volume could not trace all their connections with private and public felicity. Let it simply be asked: Where is the security for property, for reputation, for life, if the sense of religious obligation desert the oaths which are the instruments of investigation in courts of justice? And let us with caution indulge the supposition that morality can be maintained without religion. Whatever may be conceded to the influence of refined education on minds of peculiar structure, reason and experience both forbid us to expect that national morality can prevail in exclusion of religious principle.

Throughout the later part of the 20th century, and so far in the 21st century, we have seen government attempting to remove every vestige of God from the public square. If God is removed, does morality exist? Removing God from society has the immediate second and third order of effects in that it undermines religion's role in establishing a moral code, thereby leaving morality subject to popular culture and the passions of man. The thin thread that holds our republic together is the morality of you, the individual. Put another way, without God you have no religion, without religion you have no basis for morality, without morality you have no stability in law, and ultimately, you have no freedom.

Certainly, we have seen a drastic shift in the morality of our nation. In the 1960's, protestors were marching in the streets to end the war in Vietnam. They made a point of calling returning veterans "baby killers." Those protestors grew up and became politicians and then marched in the streets to support the unrestricted killing of babies in abortion clinics. President Nixon resigned in disgrace in 1974 in the face of almost certain impeachment because he lied about the break-in at the Democratic Party office. In 1998, President Clinton was impeached for lying about having sex in the Oval Office with a young staffer, yet he stayed in office.

He therefore is the truest friend to the liberty of his country who tries most to promote its virtue, and who, so far as his power and influence extend, will not suffer a man to be

chosen into any office of power and trust who
is not a wise and virtuous man . . . The sum
of all is, if we would most truly enjoy this gift
of Heaven, let us become a virtuous people.

—Samuel Adams

If you ask most Americans today if politicians are trustworthy they will respond with a chuckle as if you had lost your mind. Next ask them, "Why, then, do you trust them with your life, liberty and property?"

Thomas Jefferson wrote:

I think it lost time to attend lectures on
moral philosophy. He who made us would
have been a pitiful bungler if He had made
the rules of our moral conduct a matter of
science (i.e., knowledge acquired by
systematic study). For one man of science
there are thousands who are not. What would
have become of them? Man was formed for
society. His morality, therefore, was to be
formed to this object. He was endowed with
a sense of right and wrong, merely relative to
this. This sense is as much a part of his

nature as the sense of hearing, seeing, feeling;

it is the true foundation of morality... [2]

Our founding fathers spent a great deal of time talking about morality as the basis for the rule of law, the Constitution. Today, society avoids morality like the plague, unless emotionally charged, condemning morality as a tool of the ignorant, self-righteous, bigoted followers of ancient texts—Christians.

"What does anything that is truly beautiful lack? Nothing! No more than does moral or natural law, truth, kindness, or self-respect. Which of these is improved by praise or marred by criticism?" [3]

—Marcus Aurelius

I recently read an op-ed by Frank Bruni in the *New York Times*: "Bigotry, the Bible and the Lessons of Indiana." In this article he argues that advances in science and knowledge created a new understanding or new morality. Truly, we see a new morality in our nation.

---

[2] Andrew M. Allison, et al., *The Real Thomas Jefferson*, (National Center for Constitutional Studies, Eight Printing, 2010) 555.
[3] Marcus Aurelius, *The Emperor's Handbook*, (New York, NY: Scribner 2002) 45.

So what is it about this word that causes so much angst? *Webster's American Family Dictionary* defines morality as:

1. *Conformity to the rules of right conduct; moral or virtuous conduct.*

2. *Moral quality or character.*

3. *Virtue in sexual matters; chastity.*

4. *A doctrine or system of morals...*

Our laws were instituted on a fairly simple basis as established by the Ten Commandments, and were universally accepted as standards of morality in our nation until progressives began challenging God in the judicial system. Here is the list of those Commandments:

1. You shall have no other gods before Me.

2. You shall not make idols.

3. You shall not take the name of the Lord, your God, in vain.

4. Remember the Sabbath day, to keep it holy.

5. Honor your father and your mother.

6. You shall not murder.

7. You shall not commit adultery.

8. You shall not steal.

9. You shall not bear false witness against your neighbor.

10. You shall not covet.

Why would any moral human being have any problem with these laws in civil society? What disagreement could you find with these? Certainly, even an atheist who doesn't believe there is a God could not find argument with honoring father and mother, not stealing, lying, or murdering. God's law is unchanging, so morality based on God's law is impartial and not biased. God's morality is not subject to the whims of man or his fashionable culture. It is not enhanced by applause or degraded by ridicule. Plainly stated, it is immovable by the designs of men.

The morality of a nation should not be determined by an individual or by a theocracy. Hitler's twisted morality lead Germany to the systematic murder of six million Jews; additionally, he killed some five million others including radicals, gypsies, homosexuals, Catholics, liberals, and the mentally and/or physically disabled. Fourteen hundred years of Islamic jihad with beheadings, crucifixions, rape, and slavery show the danger of a theocracy. Government morality, or legislated morality, is about creating a collective morality. A collective government morality has no place for individual conscience, which ultimately ends in complete control of a population.

When a nation has problems today, we now have the United Nations to facilitate corrective action. Soon the 193 member nations of the United Nations will be the administrators of global morality. Think about the fact that most of these nations are run by monarchs, dictators, despots, or oligarchs who have never believed in individual freedom and decide both the morality and religion of their citizens. Morals have to come from an immovable foundation that is not subject to popular culture or the applause of the majority. If morality changes with popular culture, then in fact you have no morality—it is relative and subject only to the passions of man.

A couple of years ago I attended a presentation on the U.S. Constitution. The subject was "*Is Our Nation a Christian Nation? The Founding Fathers and Religion.*" It was given at a local university and open to the public. At the time, I was teaching classes on the Constitution and my wife convinced me that it might be an informative lecture for me to hear.

Not long after sitting down in the auditorium, my wife leaned over to me and asked if I heard what the people were talking about. She proceeded to tell me that we had come to the campus atheist club meeting. That piqued my interest. After years of my own study of the Founders, I had no doubt of their faith in God.

I was listening attentively when the professor started speaking, as I wanted to hear how he was going to address the issue. Even though the professor's bias in favor of atheism was evident, he graciously allowed a question and answer period after his discourse.

At the completion of the lecture, a number of students approached my wife and me and asked us to join the atheist club. I was a little taken aback and asked why they would want a couple of fifty year old followers-of-Jesus to join their club. They responded that they liked hearing our point of view because they "usually just get together, agree on everything, eat some donuts, and go home."

One young man came up to me and said, "*You think I'm going to hell, don't you?*" I asked him how I would know that. He then asked me what I believed, and I quoted Romans 10:9: **"If you confess with your mouth the Lord Jesus, and believe in your heart that God has raised Him from the dead, you will be saved."** He became extremely agitated and again asked me if I thought he was going to hell. I told him, "*I'm not God and have no idea where you are going, that's between you and*

God, not you and me." I added, "Listen, this wasn't a religious meeting, it was about politics. Let me ask you a question. If there was an atheist and a Christian running for a political office, whom would you vote for?" He didn't pause for a second and answered, "The Christian." It rocked me a little, and I asked why. He responded, "Because you guys believe in ultimate accountability."

Interesting that here is a professing atheist who believes his best opportunity for truth and justice come from someone who believes in ultimate accountability. He intuitively understood that man is best when he is controlled by his conscience. Conversely, without a belief in ultimate accountability, nothing would restrain the actions of man.

The second important fact in this conversation was that this young man had made a judgment based on his experience and beliefs—that he would rather have a Christian leading him than an atheist. Many people confuse morality with judging people. Although morality expressly requires you to decide and live by a set of principles, it does not put you in a position to force others to live that same way.

We as a people can ignore, belittle, and ridicule God, morality, and religion, but we do so at our own peril. We would do well to listen to those who have lived under a totalitarian regime. The following is from Alexander Solzhenitsyn's address at Templeton in 1983:

> *More than half a century ago, while I was still a child, I recall hearing a number of older people offer the following explanation for the great disasters that had befallen Russia: Men have forgotten God; that's why all this has happened.*

> *Since then I have spent well-nigh fifty years working on the history of our Revolution; in the process I have read hundreds of books, collected hundreds of personal testimonies, and have already contributed eight volumes of my own toward the effort of clearing away the rubble left by that upheaval. But if I were asked today to formulate as concisely as possible the main cause of the ruinous Revolution that swallowed up some sixty million of our people, I could not put it more accurately than to repeat: Men have forgotten God; that's why all this has happened.*

What is more, the events of the Russian Revolution can only be understood now, at the end of the century, against the background of what has since occurred in the rest of the world. What emerges here is a process of universal significance. And if I were called upon to identify briefly the principal trait of the entire twentieth century, here too, I would be unable to find anything more precise and pithy than to repeat once again: Men have forgotten God.

You can restore a nation, but it starts and ends with your individual morality. Psalm 51: "*Create in me a clean heart, O God, and renew a steadfast spirit in me.*" You can't change your spouse, children, or neighbor. You can, however, run your own self-government with integrity, honor, courage, and commitment. People do not begrudge leaders their positions of authority nor even the perks that go with the job unless they believe that their leaders are immoral, unethical, or tyrants. Whether you lead one or many, here is a simple way to restore civility in our nation—it is found in the Bible, Matthew 22:37:

Jesus replied, 'You must love the Lord your God with all your heart, all your soul, and all your mind.' This is the first and greatest commandment. A second is equally important: 'Love you neighbor as yourself'. The entire law and all the prophets are based on these two commandments.

Arm yourself for action with these two thoughts: first, do only what your sovereign and lawgiving reason tells you is for the good of others; and second, do not hesitate to change course if someone is able to show you where you are mistaken or point out a better way. But be persuaded only by arguments based on justice and the common good, never by what appeals to your taste for pleasure or popularity. [4]

—Marcus Aurelius

---

[4] Aurelius, *The Emperor's Handbook*, 44.

Courage

"Courage is contagious. When a brave man takes a stand, the spines of others are often stiffened."

—Billy Graham

July 2, 1776, was a warm day in Philadelphia, but the temperature had nothing to do with the heated exchange that was taking place among the 56 men from the thirteen colonies who debated the Declaration of Independence in the Philadelphia State House. Thomas Jefferson, the author of the Declaration of Independence, sat quietly by as these men decided the future of their relationship with the British Crown. On July 4, the delegates approved the Declaration, and the president of the Continental Congress, John Hancock, signed it. It wouldn't be until August 2 that all delegates completed the signing. This was no trivial matter for the gathering of farmers, merchants, plantation owners, and lawyers. They knew that signing the Declaration meant they were signing their death warrants as traitors to Great Britain and would result in mortal combat with the most powerful army and navy the world had known.

The last sentence reads, *"And for the support of this Declaration, with a firm reliance on the protection of divine Providence, we mutually pledge to each other our Lives, our Fortunes and our sacred Honor."* As Benjamin Franklin was signing the Declaration of Independence, he said, *"We must all hang together or we will surely hang separately."* They held to their pledge, though many did not live to see the outcome. Some lost family, some lost homes and fortunes, five were captured by the British, tortured, and died, and nine fought and died during the war. They had no idea the cost they were about to pay or that the war would grind on until the Peace of Paris was signed on September 3, 1783. They were common men with uncommon courage who put their lives on the line for the dream of freedom from tyranny.

"I am more afraid of an army of 100 sheep led by a lion than an army of 100 lions led by a sheep."
—Talleyrand

Contrast the courage of our founders, who were willing to put it all on the line for the belief in an ideal known as freedom, with an emasculated America we see today. Most people in the United States today are motivated more by fear than courage. Political correctness has stood in direct opposition to the truth for a generation. Powerful words such as bigot, racist, homophobe, and Islamophobe have been used to suppress truth and establish a false doctrine destructive to the future of our nation.

Courage, honor, integrity—three values infused in past generations—have largely been bred out of today's generations. Clever campaigns of political correctness have been designed to silence all opposition in order to control your thoughts, speech, and action. Today, people live in fear of the government, fear of special interest groups, and fear of the media. The childhood saying of old, *"sticks and stones may break my bones, but words will never hurt me"* could be translated today as *"sticks and stones may break my bones, but words can kill me."*

In our society today we have distressing, absurd situations, such as the case of a young boy who is expelled from elementary school for pointing his finger and gesturing as if firing a gun. I have never known a boy who has not performed that same action at some point, even when they were raised by families that possessed no guns. It is part of their nature, but we Americans have let radical progressives suppress the nature of those boys as something harmful or unnatural. Meanwhile, the same progressives think it natural to read a book on transgender indoctrination to children in an elementary school entitled, "*I Am Jazz*," a book about a boy who wants to be a girl. Contrast that with what happened to the company that produces Clorox Bleach. Clorox has been "turning things white" for decades, but the company recently had to apologize and explain that it wasn't racist.

Feminism is defined as a range of movements and ideologies that share a common goal: to define, establish, and achieve equal political, economic, cultural, personal, and social rights for women. It is a movement seeking to establish equal opportunities for women in education and employment. A feminist advocates or supports the rights and equality of women. Self-proclaimed feminists in our society are quick to attack mainstream Christian values as a "war on women," yet they are silent about child brides, female genital mutilation, rape, women being considered chattel, and slavery espoused by Islam.

There are also those who legitimately disagree with a politician's stance on any issue, but do not voice their opinion unless he is a white male for fear of being labeled a racist or sexist, or sometimes both. A book could be written about the attempts to demonize traditional values that most Americans hold true.

You need to stand up and defend your beliefs before you are not allowed to have any. By standing today, you will encourage your neighbor to stand up tomorrow. It will take courage.

"Have I not commanded you? Be strong and of good courage; do not be afraid, nor dismayed, for the Lord your God is with you wherever you go."
—Joshua 1:9

We as a culture celebrate heroes who display courage in the face of extreme danger, as well we should—the military person who goes above and beyond the call of duty risking life and limb to save someone, the policeman, fireman, or neighbor who saves someone's life from certain destruction when an unexpected event occurs. We honor the person who does not hesitate, but sacrifices all for stranger or friend. This type of courage is called physical courage; no planning or preparation can prepare you for your response. In the Marine Corps, we can train two people exactly alike, and one can end up a hero and the other a zero at the point of testing. All men dream of being a hero. As little boys they tie towels around their necks and pretend to be superheroes; as old men they still dream of saving someone's life—it's just the way they are made. The truth is, though, most men will go through life without their physical courage ever being tested.

An iconic example of physical courage took place in China on the June 5, 1989. After almost seven weeks of pro-democracy protests by students, the Chinese government moved in to crush the protest in Tiananmen Square. Hundreds of protestors were killed on the third and fourth of June. On the fifth of June a column of tanks was moving down the street and a man armed with nothing more than a couple of shopping bags stepped in front of the tanks to stop them. When they tried to go around him he jumped into their way, eventually jumping on the tank and yelling at them. The "Tank Man" is a lasting symbol of physical courage—in a moment where death was certain this man stepped in to stop the slaughter.

There is, however, another type of courage that everyone is tested with; it is called moral courage. Moral courage is different in that it is always premeditated. You always have the opportunity to stand up and do the right thing for the right reason. Should you fail, moral courage empowers you to go back and make it right. Moral courage is probably the single most important ingredient of effective leadership and restoration in our nation.

Peer pressure is a tool as powerful on the playground as it is in the boardroom, school board, city council, or state legislature. Nobody wants to be wrong, belittled, or ridiculed for his or her expressed viewpoint, thoughts, or beliefs. The truth is, though, for everyone who has the boldness to speak the truth, there is an army of people who wished they had the guts to do the same.

As a leader, your moral courage will be tested almost daily. For instance, your boss comes up with a plan he falls in love with and your peers, the 'yes' men, jump on board. You see a fatal flaw and are left to swim against the current of popular thought and point out why the plan will not succeed. You have subordinates who willfully disregard policy: Do you pretend you didn't see it? You have an employee who needs to be fired for the good of the organization: Do you take care of it or just have them transferred to become someone else's problem?

Many of us have recently viewed videos produced by Center for Medical Progress in which Planned Parenthood leadership casually discusses selling the body parts of aborted babies like crop futures. Many of our elected representatives in

Congress lack the moral courage to defend the first unalienable right—the right to life. Do you believe this practice to be immoral? If you do, as a citizen of this nation, it is your duty, your right, and your privilege to stand up for that belief. It can simply start with a call, email, or letter to government representatives to get them to stop taxpayer funding of Planned Parenthood when they have irrefutable evidence of illegal, immoral, and unethical behavior.

Our country is dying for want of leaders in all walks of life who are willing to speak the truth with boldness. Aristotle said, *"You will never do anything in this world without courage. It is the greatest quality of the mind next to honor."*

We need many with the faith and courage of our country's founders to once again stand up in the face of evil and speak. Dietrich Bonhoeffer, a German pastor in his twenties, stood against Hitler and his final solution for the Jewish race. He was eventually imprisoned and executed three weeks before Hitler committed suicide and the war ended. He said, *"Silence in the face of evil is itself evil. God will not hold us guiltless. Not to speak is to speak. Not to act is to act."*

Leadership always requires courage—it required courage in 1776, and it requires courage today. Leadership does not compromise principle, it does not tolerate injustice, and it makes no accommodation for evil. Courage is a decision. Leaders who know what is right and take a stand in defense of their convictions will always have their moral courage tested.

We don't lack heroes who are willing to sacrifice life and limb to save another—we lack those who are willing to sacrifice their peaceful coexistence to do the right thing. Moral courage is standing when no one is standing with you.

The Home Front

"Train up a child in the way he should go, and when he is old he will not depart from it."

—Proverbs 22:6

Here is a law of nature that is irrefutable: leadership vacuums do not exist anywhere in nature. If you do not lead your children, they will lead you. If you do not lead, they will look for someone else to lead them, and that is generally a path you do not want them travelling.

There is nothing easy about being a parent. It is, without a doubt, one of the toughest jobs in the world. Once you start, there is no turning back. You, like everyone else, want excellence in your children, but excellence is not an accident. It starts with standards and it ends with standards. You can let society, the government, or the public school system determine standards for your children, or you can choose to be the leader of your home and determine the standards. You would do well to remember this: they will always aspire to the honorable traits demonstrated by caring parents.

As I look at life today, I sometimes think I must have grown up in a parallel universe. We were taught at home to respect our elders. Today you can go into a store, restaurant, school, or just about anywhere else and see out-of-control children who are running, screaming, and using foul language, and parents standing by in a state of shell-shock, begging their little ones to behave. You may also see another kind of parent standing by with adoring doe eyes while their out-of-control children run rampant through a store ransacking shelves. These parents act as though their children are the cutest things anyone has ever seen, and are completely unaware the rest of the world does not find them charming at all.

Anyone who has raised children has had those moments when their kids have gone off the rails in public. As an example, a few years ago, we were having breakfast in a restaurant and our youngest decided to become the center of attention in the restaurant. After a warning and no corresponding change in behavior, I took her to the car and adjusted her attitude. We returned and she was well-behaved. We were sitting next to an older couple and when we finished eating, the woman leaned over to my wife and said, "*Thank you. Most parents just let their kids act up in public and disrupt everyone's meal.*" The solution is never to let children decide when their disruptive behavior will end. As a child, I would have never considered acting that way in public, and I wasn't an anomaly. Everyone I knew was raised in a similar fashion and acted accordingly.

In our day, we were like every other child—on the prowl looking for trouble to get into, and we usually found it. However, if an adult caught us in our wayward wanderings, they would pull us up short with a warning, "*Do you want me to call your dad?*" We were taught to respect adults, and talking back to them wasn't even a thought. We knew they had some type of secret network, and if you got out of line with one, you were going to be in trouble when you got home. Today, most adults are afraid of correcting these children for fear of retribution from either the child or the child's parents.

We were taught to respect authority. When we went to school, the teachers and school administrators were the law. The common knowledge was that if we got in trouble at school, it would be doubled at home. I was a slow learner and spent plenty of time in trouble at both places. Occasionally, of course, the teacher was wrong, but that did not prevent me from being disciplined. If I could prove without a shadow of doubt I was innocent, I would still get the lecture about who was in charge, and it was not me.

The police and sheriff's deputies? They were never wrong—when they said, "*Jump*," we asked, "*How high?*" As we got older and bolder, some of our mischief could have resulted in an arrest, however the peace officers opted to let us go home and face the wrath of our parents.

Society, as a whole, seemed a lot more stable in my youth. The older the person, the more respect was accorded to them. It certainly did not mean we agreed with the older folks in our lives—it just meant that we respected them. We were taught simple things like opening doors for women, firm handshakes, and pleasant greetings when interacting with someone older. Those were all lessons I first learned at home and lessons that were reinforced in the community. We have certainly evolved, but not in a good way.

"Respect for ourselves guides our morals; respect for others guides our manners."
—Laurence Sterne

Today's news offers a different view of society. We see flash mobs of teenagers robbing stores; we are assaulted by unrestricted use of foul language in public, and kids tragically ending the lives of their peers. When we witness respect for authority, elders, and private property from youth today, it is both surprising and noteworthy.

While in the Marine Corps, I had the opportunity to work with one of the finest leaders I have ever known, Sergeant Major (SgtMaj) L.P. Fineran. Two things set him apart from other leaders I have known—respect and courtesy. At the time, I was the battalion commander of Marines who had recently returned from combat and were preparing for the next combat tour.

By the time SgtMaj Fineran arrived at the battalion, he had already attained the highest enlisted rank in the Marine Corps, and respect was something he had both earned and deserved. However, he used his position of authority not to gain respect but to give respect. His respect flowed from common principles of decency and courtesy. When we would walk through the battalion area, he would see a Marine and say, "*Good morning Marine, how are you doing?*" The Marine might respond, "*Good morning, SgtMaj. Fine.*" SgtMaj Fineran would then stop and ask, "*How about me?*" The Marine might then reply, "*SgtMaj?*" He would ask, "*Well, how am I doing? I asked you about yourself. What about me?*" If he walked into a room and was shaking hands and someone decided not to stand up to shake hands, he would simply say, "*Get up off your butt if you want to shake my hand.*" His example became infectious. Common courtesy and respect fundamentally transformed our unit more effectively than anything I had experienced in twenty prior years of service.

SgtMaj Fineran might not have been liked by everyone, but he was respected by everyone because he always set the example of respect and common courtesy. If you want your kids to respect others, set the example and teach them respect at home and they will not disappoint you in public.

> **"*Never act without purpose and resolve, or without the means to finish the job.*"[5]**
> —Marcus Aurelius

SgtMaj Fineran came into my office frequently to reaffirm, "*Sir, it's all about standards.*" Not surprisingly, we had many standards in the Marine Corps—proven standards that

---

[5] Aurelius, *The Emperor's Handbook*, 41.

were meant to create excellence in the organization. The problem was not the standards themselves but the enforcement of those standards. You see, we all have standards that are more important to us than others. We knowingly or unknowingly overlook things that we don't believe are important.

Once you, as the leader, selectively disregard standards because they are unpopular or old-fashioned, your children will respond in kind and follow your example. And, before long, there is a snowball effect and you are at a loss as to where to start addressing the problem.

The basic unit of a society and a nation is the family. You can fix the nation but it starts with the family. There is no such thing as the perfect parent or the perfect child. Having been both a child and a parent, I can attest to failing time and again. Failure, however, is not an excuse for inaction. There are no guarantees that your children will not make poor choices. I made mistakes but my parents instilled in me a sense of right and wrong, of respect and courtesy. Rooted in their teachings, as I grew older I chose to follow their examples and live my life aligned with the standards that were set for me by my parents.

Concern for proper development and well-being of all individuals involved needs to be the driving factor in standards—

not control. Every organization has standards: standards of conduct, standards of quality, and production standards, both written and unwritten. Organizations usually do not fail because they lack standards; they usually fail because of the lack of enforcement of standards. It is the same in a home—only you are the one who will decide the standards. You have to be the leader who has the moral courage and the commitment to enforce those standards. Furthermore, you must be the one who does not violate those standards. *"Do as I say, not as I do"* does not work.

Will you fail? Possibly. Will your kids turn out just the way you wanted? Maybe not. Just decide to give them the best possible foundation while they are in your care. There are no promises that your children will turn out the way you wanted or never violate the principles and standards that you set for them. You only have one promise: when they are old, they will return to what you taught them. The home is where you can start the restoration of our nation.

The Public School System

"I don't send my kids to school to be socialized—that's my
job. I send them to be educated."

—Unknown

"Free education for all children in public schools. Abolition
of children's factory labor in its present form. Combination
of education with industrial production."

#10 of 'The Ten Planks of the Communist Manifesto'

—Karl Marx

In the early history of our nation, schools were
established at the local level and funded by the parents of
students. Children were taught reading, writing, and arithmetic.
Many children were home schooled, and of course, some
children received no schooling. The *Federalist Papers* were
written in 1787-1788 and anonymously appeared in New York
newspapers. The average citizen who had received a tenth grade

education was able to read and understand them. Today, university students find them too complicated. I recently watched a clip of a Texas Tech University student asking other college students simple questions like, "Who won the civil war?" "What nation did we win our independence from?" "Who is the Vice-President of the United States?" Sadly, most did not have a clue.

As a disclaimer, this chapter is not intended to be an indictment against teachers or administrators in any way. Most are hard-working, thoroughly dedicated professionals who have made a difference in the lives of students. Most of us can recall a teacher who made a critical and life-changing difference in our lives. This is simply an indictment against government-run education, which has tied the hands of those professionals through legislation and regulation.

The federal government did not start funding public education until the early 1900's. Sadly, it did not take long for the government to gain complete control of the education system in the nation. In 1965, President Johnson signed the Elementary and Secondary Education Act into law, fully cementing government control of public education. President Carter created the Department of Education in 1979.

The U.S. Constitution gives the federal government no authority to collect taxes for, fund, or operate schools. Therefore, under the Tenth Amendment, education should be entirely a state and local matter. For more than 200 years, the federal government had left education to those who were in the best position to oversee it—state and local governments and families. Richard L. Lyman, president of Stanford University, who testified at the congressional hearings on forming the new department, pointed out that "the two-hundred-year-old absence of the Department of Education is not the result of simple failure during all that time. On the contrary, it derives from the conviction that we do not want the kind of educational system that such arrangements produce. [6]

In 1979, the Department of Education opened with a $14 billion budget; by 2014, the Department's budget was $67.3

---

[6] David Salisbury, Cato Handbook for Congress Policy Recommendations for the 108th Congress, Cato Institute Washington, D.C.

billion. The cost of public education is largely funded by state and local governments, but the combined total in 1964 was $27.2 billion; in 2010, the total was $919.7 billion.

In spite of the shocking and skyrocketing increase in the cost of public education, in 2012 the United States education system ranked 36 out of 65 nations taking the International Student Assessment.[7]

The cost to run the Department of Education continues to rise and is predicted to continue to escalate. The price of education has risen more since 1965 than the cost of health care, yet nobody is asking to reduce spending on education. In conjunction with the rise in cost is the decline of performance. The cost of education is out of control and the solution is not more money; it is returning the schools to local control. The government solution to any problem is more money, more personnel, and more control.

In 2010, the New York school system was paying 550 teachers $30 million each year to sit in "Rubber Rooms" and do nothing while awaiting case dispositions between the teachers'

---

[7] Julia Ryan, "American Schools vs. the World: Expensive, Unequal, Bad at Math," *The Atlantic*, Dec 3, 2013.

union and the school.[8] Administrators are restrained from relieving the system of incompetent teachers by unions, even as the public continues to pay those teachers' salaries.

Schools, like businesses, are better served by local free market principles with consumers determining quality rather than the government doing so. If schools began to compete for students based on performance, rest assured that the education system would improve. Promotion and retention would be based on performance rather than union membership. The government mandated school system is one of the few places in America where someone is given a job for life after reaching tenure, performance being irrelevant.

> *"I think we risk becoming the best informed society that has ever died of ignorance."*
> —Reuben Blades

Today's public school system has become as much about social engineering as about education. As an example: Horace Mitchell Primary School in Kittery Point, Maine, was recently featured in the news when school officials decided to read a book to students titled, "*I Am Jazz*". The book is about a transgender

---

[8] Jennifer Media, "Teachers Set Deal with City on Discipline Process," *The New York Times*, April 15, 2010.

child "with a boy's body and a girl's brain."[9] One parent was understandably upset when her seven-year-old son came home and wondered if he might be "trans-something," a subject of which he had no previous knowledge.

"The first gold star a child gets in school for the mere performance of a needful task is its first lesson in graft."
—Philip Wylie, *Generation of Vipers*, 1942

After my mom died, we were sorting through stuff when my wife came across a Punt, Pass, and Kick trophy I won as a young boy. It was a third place trophy—she wanted to keep it and I wanted to throw it away; I considered it a trophy for the second loser. Today's system of rewarding every child who participates in any activity with a trophy is a great reminder that sits in contrast with today's world. Self-esteem need not be earned; everyone is a winner. We handicap kids when we stop allowing them to compete in this world. They will be sadly disappointed when they start working and find out that there are no rewards for showing up to work and doing what they were

---

[9] David McCormack, "School Officials Under Fire for Reading Transgender Children's Book to Kindergartners Without Telling Their Parents," *Daily Mail,* last modified April 20, 2015, http://www.dailymail.co.uk/news/article-3047492/School-fire-reading-transgender-children-s-book-kindergarteners-without-telling-parents.html

hired to do. Self-respect and self-esteem have to be earned if they are ever going to be of any value. In real life not everyone gets a trophy. As a nation we need to raise young people to be competitive and self-reliant, not to be wards of the state.

Anyone who is paying attention realizes that the government-run school system is failing. That is why so many parents are looking at school choice, private schools, or homeschooling options. Even the government recognizes it is failing to produce acceptable results —that is why we have had so many different programs in recent years: *No Child Left Behind*, *Race to the Top*, and now *Common Core*.

Common Core is an interesting social engineering program designed to pigeonhole your child in a predetermined career market.

> *The standards were drafted by experts and teachers from across the country and are designed to ensure students are prepared for today's entry-level careers, freshman-level college courses, and workforce training programs . . . The new standards also provide a way for teachers to measure student progress throughout the school year and*

ensure that students are on the pathway to success in their academic careers.

—*Common Core* (corestandards.org)

A recent article featured in Glenn Beck's online news source, *The Blaze*, further shows how *Common Core* intentionally socially engineers children as reflected in the following cause and effect lesson:

> *One day some time ago, a boy named Jack was doing his homework. His mother began to examine Jack's textbook. A puzzled look clouded her face. She noticed that the book was worn and missing a dozen pages. The next day, she told the school's principal that Jack deserved better materials. He agreed, but said that only schools in white districts got new texts. Schools in African American areas got old damaged books.*[10]

---

[10] Mike Opelka, "Common Core-Related Worksheet Teaches That Only White Schools Get New Textbooks," *The Blaze* May 5, 2015, http://www.theblaze.com/stories/2015/05/05/common-core-related-worksheet-teaches-that-only-white-schools-get-new-textbooks/

Social engineering does not stop with *Common Core*. Recently the Fairfax County School Board in Fairfax, Virginia, voted to expand its nondiscrimination policy to accommodate transgender teachers and students. While parents overwhelmingly disapproved, the school board chairwoman released a statement explaining they had no choice: *"The U.S. Department of Education has told school districts that transgender students are protected from discrimination under Title IX and has recently required some school districts including Alexandria, Va., to amend their policies to expressly include gender identity."* [11] In other words, the government would withhold funds unless the school supported the administration's agenda on nondiscrimination for transgender students and teachers.

It doesn't stop there, however—it is also a powerful tool designed to collect hundreds of data points of personal and private information from students and also from students' families. Ultimately, *Common Core* is an assault on the privacy of public school students and their families by the federal government. *"What kinds of data are we talking about? The*

---

[11] Greg Corombos, "Obama to Schools: Gender-Bend or Lose Funding," *World Net Daily* May 9, 2015, http://www.wnd.com/2015/05/obama-to-schools-gender-bend-or-lose-funding/.

National Education Data Model includes over 400 data points, including health history, disciplinary history, family income range, voting status, religious affiliation, and on and on." [12]

Undoubtedly, most of the data collected will be monetized; it will be sold to corporations for targeted advertising and economic exploitation. However, *Common Core's* data mining takes on Orwellian principles in that it looks for information long held to be personal, private, and out of government reach, such as health history, income, voting status, and religious affiliation. The question has to be asked: Why has it become essential to the education of our children?

Karl Marx and fellow communists knew that public education was one of the most historically proven ways to eventually control a society. For almost 200 years the federal government did not control the education system. Was the education better or worse? Article 1, section 8, of the Constitution granted Congress eighteen specific powers, and education was not one of them.

---

[12] Jane Robbins, "Common Core & Data Collection," *Truth in American Education* April 7, 2014, http://truthinamericaneducation.com/privacy-issues-state-longitudinal-data-system/common-core-data-collection/.

To ensure the restoration of our nation, it is imperative for our education system to be returned to local and parental control. Education functions best when education is locally controlled and evaluated by local parents. You are the only one who is concerned about the quality of education your child receives—you are the only one who can influence the outcome.

The Church and State

"I know your works, that you are neither cold nor hot. I could wish you were cold or hot. So then, because you are lukewarm, and neither cold nor hot, I will vomit you out of My mouth."

—Revelation 3:15-16

In order to talk about church and government, we first need to debunk a myth: "Separation of church and state" is not found anywhere in the Constitution of the United States. It was a doctrine that came from a letter Thomas Jefferson wrote to a committee of the Danbury Baptist association in Connecticut in 1802. The Danbury Baptist association was concerned that the government might legislate laws that would restrict the free exercise of religion. In Jefferson's reply, he stated, *"I contemplate with sovereign reverence that act of the whole American people which declared that their legislature would 'make no law respecting an establishment of religion, or*

65

prohibiting the free exercise thereof,' thus building a wall of separation between Church and State."

For an in-depth analysis of this issue, I recommend reading the article written by David Barton titled *The Separation of Church and State.* .

The Declaration of Independence mentions God four times. The First Amendment to the Constitution states, **"Congress shall make no law respecting an establishment of religion, or prohibiting the free exercise thereof; or abridging the freedom of speech or of the press; or the right of the people peaceably to assemble, and to petition the government for a redress of grievances."** Churches met in government buildings across the states, and even the United States Capitol served as a church building until after the civil war.[13]

Alexis de Tocqueville, noted French political thinker and historian, spent nine months in the United States observing the new republic in 1831. He wrote in *Democracy in America,* **"The Americans combine the notions of Christianity and of liberty so intimately in their minds, that it is impossible to**

---

[13] David Barton, "Church in the U.S. Capitol," *Wallbuilders* November 10, 2005, http://www.wallbuilders.com/libissuesarticles.asp?id=90

make them conceive the one without the other..." In Book Two of *Democracy in America* he wrote, "*Christianity has therefore retained a strong hold on the public mind in America . . . In the United States . . . Christianity itself is a fact so irresistibly established, that no one undertakes either to attack or to defend it.*"[14]

George Washington said, "*Of all the dispositions and habits which lead to political prosperity, religion and morality are indispensable supports.*" John Adams wrote, "*Our Constitution was made only for a moral and religious people. It is wholly inadequate to the government of any other.*" It would be foolish to claim that the United States was anything but a Christian nation at its founding, where church and state were interconnected as well as cohesive components critical to the success of a government—of the people, by the people, for the people.

The founders came to the new world for freedom of religion. The United States was formed in the churches, and wrongs perpetrated by the government were addressed in the

---

[14] Bill Federer, "Alexis de Tocqueville-Christianity in the United States, Islam in Algeria & How America Would End," *American Minute* April 16, 2015, http://www.americanminute.com/index.php?date=04-16&view=View.

churches. In 1954 the "Johnson amendment" was passed, which was an attempt to silence the speakers in the pulpit from addressing Scriptural truth in relation to candidates for political office. Today, tax law clearly cements the connection of church and state. Churches are required to file as 501C (3) tax-exempt organizations. The government has threatened churches with losing their tax-exempt status if they engaged or supported political positions. Only a politician would attempt to silence the church through fear and intimidation by proposing tax law legislation—the very thing which the Danbury Baptists feared. If you can silence the church you can control the nation.

The very people who espouse the separation of church and state are the ones who want to ensure government control over the churches. The new mantra used by politicians supports the "freedom to worship" versus the "freedom of religion" that the Constitution prescribes. "Freedom to worship" connotates that people can do what they want inside a church, but *not outside* a church building. The government has already changed "freedom of religion" to "freedom of worship." The U.S. Citizen and Immigration Services civics test, for those seeking citizenship, asks which rights are guaranteed by the Constitution. The correct answer is "freedom to worship," not "freedom of religion."[15] If the church remains silent, it will become "hate speech" to fulfill the "Great Commission"—to preach the gospel to the world.

A military chaplain was recently relieved of his position because he used Scripture as the basis for counseling sailors who came to him for counseling. This is nothing new in the armed forces. The government has continued to attempt to restrict what ordained Christian chaplains can say. When I was a battalion commander a few years ago, the Navy said chaplains could not pray at official functions using the name of Jesus.

I asked my chaplain if he was a Christian, to which he replied that he was. I asked him if he believed that Jesus was the Son of God and that He came to earth, died, and rose again for the remission of his sins, and again he answered, "Yes." I told him, "Very well, then I don't want to hear prayers to the god of the wind, rocks, trees or grass; I want to hear them to God." I also told him not to worry—if anyone was going to get relieved it would be me, not him. I explained that since we were getting ready to deploy back to a combat zone, the Marines and Sailors

---

[15] Kelsey Harkness, "US Immigration Exam Replaces 'Freedom of Religion' with 'Freedom of Worship'," *The Daily Signal* April 30, 2015, http://dailysignal.com/2015/04/30/republican-senator-questions-why-immigration-exam calls-freedom-of-religion-freedom-of-worship/

needed to know that he believed because he would probably be the first to have them knocking on his door for counsel in tough situations.

I recently heard a speech by Hillary Clinton, a presidential candidate, where she said, *"Deep-seated cultural codes, religious beliefs and structural biases have to be changed."* More and more, the government and politicians want to determine what our religious beliefs should or should not be. They want Christians to ignore the Word of God as prescribed in the Bible and let the government and popular culture determine our moral code rather than God.

"Just as Death and Destruction are never satisfied, so human desire is never satisfied."
—Proverbs 27:20

The moral code for a society and nation is either going to come from the government or the church. History is a grim reminder of moral codes being established by the government. Oligarchies, dictators, communists, and fascists have killed and enslaved millions under their "moral" code of right and wrong.

The founders were adamantly opposed to state religions. They saw first-hand how state religion was a powerful tool in the hands of government to restrict the God-given rights to life, liberty, and private property ownership. They also understood how state religion would be powerful enough to indeed force an individual to violate his/her conscience. Thomas Jefferson said, *"No provision in our Constitution ought to be dearer to man than that which protects the rights of conscience."*

Established theocracies are a prime example of how deadly and restrictive a government can be of personal freedoms and private property ownership. Today, we see the continuation of 1400 years of jihad by the Muslims. That theocracy kills all non-Muslims, and Muslims who aren't good-enough Muslims— beheading and crucifying them. They believe women and children are chattel, they kill homosexuals, condone female genital mutilation, child brides, and slavery. No, we do not want a theocracy.

The church can no longer divorce itself from society and its responsibility to good government. The founders understood that true liberty came from a moral and religious people, not from the laws of a nation. The government has banished God from the public square. The public school system has become the biggest purveyor of godless ethics, and the church has become an emasculated body that cowers in fear of any adverse public opinion.

The Supreme Court has decided for homosexual marriage. Clearly, the government is saying to the church that marriage is between man and state, not man and God. A pastor licensed by the state will then be required to perform homosexual marriages, just as bakers who have been forced to make cakes, or photographers who have been forces to take pictures. If the Supreme Court decides what marriage is, rather than God, pastors should simply unhinge themselves from state control by relinquishing their ability to perform marriages. They should instead perform "religious ceremonies" for members within the church—free from government control—not unlike communion, baptism and funerals.

The church is to judge actions, not people—it would do well to look at the example Jesus left with us. This is the story of a woman who was caught in the act of adultery. The religious leaders brought her to Jesus:

> '*The law of Moses says to stone her. What do you say?'* . . . *They kept demanding an answer, so He stood up again and said, 'All right, but let the one who has never sinned*

throw the first stone!' . . . When the accusers
heard this, they slipped away one by one,
beginning with the oldest, until only Jesus
was left in the middle of the crowd with the
woman. Then Jesus stood up again and said
to the woman, 'Where are your accusers?
Didn't even one of them condemn you?' 'No,
Lord,' she said. And Jesus said, 'Neither do I.
Go and sin no more.'

—John: 5-11

He did not excuse her behavior; He did not tell her to go her way and not get caught again. He addressed sin but did not condemn her. If the church is silent, then man will determine the moral code of the day. Recent surveys of people in the United States reported that 83 percent of the American people identify themselves as Christians. We see little moral restraint manifested by humans in their lives. We see zero accountability for politicians who lie, steal, abuse power, and trample on the Constitution. Where is the church in all of this?

The church is the last organization which has not completely compromised its moral authority. Judgment needs to begin in the house of God; if it does not, there is no salvation for

73

our nation. The time has come for the church to stand up and begin to educate our nation on God's word and principles rather than relinquishing those to popular culture and political pressure. Our nation would change course quickly if the churches in America started relating Scriptural truth to politicians and political activity. The church is the most powerful independent voting block; if members were properly informed, they would stand against the tyranny that will certainly destroy our nation.

> *If you fail under pressure, your strength is too small. Rescue those who are unjustly sentenced to die; save them as they stagger to their death. Don't excuse yourself by saying, 'Look, we didn't know.' For God understands all hearts, and He sees you. He who guards your soul knows you knew. He will repay all people as their actions deserve.*
> —Proverbs 24:10-12

In God's world, there is no collective morality brought about by the designs of men that protects the individual from accountability to God.

"If My people who are called by My name will humble themselves and pray and seek My face and turn from their

wicked ways, I will hear from heaven and will forgive their
sins and restore their land."

—2 Chronicles 7:14

The church was called to be compassionate; it was not called to compromise. The road to hell is paved with compromise. The church is not the government and the government is not the conscience of the church. The church is not here as a theocracy to tell the government what it can and cannot do. And the government is not a dictatorship over the church to tell it what it can and cannot say. The church's responsibility is to stand up and teach biblical principles and speak biblical truth. If the government is wrong, the church should be the first to speak up. If candidates and politicians do not support biblical principles, then, like the Black Robe Regiment who spoke truth from the pulpit during our founding days, the church leaders should educate their members on the voting decisions of the politicians. If the government sanctions and spends tax dollars to promote and perform abortions, should the church remain silent? If a politician supports abortion should the church remain silent? Who, then, is the voice of conscience speaking for those without a voice?

The most powerful unifying force in the United States is the Christian church. The church can no longer remain silent to the issues that destroy nations. The church will not be held guiltless in the affairs of state. The church can no longer treat politics as a dirty business unworthy of its attention. Many in the church stay home from voting because they have no legitimate choices who share their values. Passive resistance is not an option. There are no leadership vacuums in nature; someone will lead. The church will either lead or be led; it will either speak or be silenced. It is time to actively seek and promote those individuals who represent your values and have them represent you and be your voice for positive change in your local, state, and national elections. A choice of silence today will ensure your voice will be permanently silenced tomorrow.

You need to be a voice in your church. You need to support your church leaders who are bold enough to speak. Only you can humble yourself and pray. It does not matter what others do; God says, "*If __My__ people who are called by __My__ name...*"

Government

"We hold these truths to be self-evident, that all men are created equal, that they are endowed by their Creator with certain unalienable Rights, that among these are Life, Liberty and the pursuit of Happiness . . . That to secure these rights, Governments are instituted among Men, deriving their just powers from the consent of the governed..."
—Declaration of Independence

The reason we form governments among men is to protect unalienable rights of life, liberty, and the pursuit of happiness. Unalienable rights are defined as: *"not alienable; not transferable to another or capable of being repudiated."* Simply put, the government cannot take away your rights to life, liberty, and the pursuit of happiness because they come from God.

The Constitution gave the federal government eighteen specific limited powers, in Article 1, Section 8, of the Constitution. All other powers were given to the people and the states. The Bill of Rights (the first 10 Amendments to the Constitution) was written to protect the rights given to the people—rights designed to restrict the actions of government.

After years of analyzing information as an intelligence officer in the United States Marine Corps, I learned that anomalies do occur, but when they repeat themselves it is not a coincidence, it is a trend; trends identify long-term patterns of behavior. The government in the United States has become a living organism—not unlike a swarm of locusts—that has descended on the American people devouring all subsistence, crushing hope for a better future, and representing only those with enough money to influence elections, leaving a swath of national destruction in its path.

When the majority of the American people want the national debt reduced, politicians from both parties spend more. When the majority of American people want the borders secured, politicians from both parties fund an executive order to open the doors. When the people clearly do not want universal health care, politicians from both parties ensure it will survive in perpetuity. The clear trend is that representatives from both parties no longer represent the American people.

In the 1970's and 1980's, communism was the evil empire that our nation designed the military to fight and protect our people against. Communism was the antithesis to the United States. Consider The Ten Planks of the Communist Manifesto by Karl Marx:

1. Abolition of private property, and the application of all rents of land to public purposes.

2. A heavy progressive or graduated income tax.

3. Abolition of all right of inheritance.

4. Confiscation of the property of all emigrants and rebels.

5. Centralization of credit in the hands of the state, by means of a national bank with state capital and an exclusive monopoly.

6. Centralization of the means of communications and transportation in the hands of the State.

7. Extension of factories and instruments of production owned by the state, the bringing into cultivation of wastelands, and the improvement of the soil generally in accordance with a common plan.

8. Equal obligation of all work. Establishment of industrial armies, especially for agriculture.

9. Combination of agriculture with manufacturing industries, gradual abolition of the distinction between town and country, by a more equitable distribution of population over the country.

10. Free education for all children in public schools. Abolition of children's factory labor in its present form. Combination of education with industrial production.

With each passing year, the "land of the free" is beginning to look more and more like the "land of the enslaved." It is startling how many of the 10 planks of communism have become a reality in the United States through progressive legislation.

With very few exceptions, private property ownership is merely an illusion. If you truly owned your property, you would not be forced to pay taxes on it under the threat of government confiscation. You would be allowed to pass it to your children without penalty of inheritance tax (abolition of all right of inheritance). We have a heavily progressive and graduated income tax system. Simply put, the rich pay more and the poor pay little or nothing based on income levels. The Federal Reserve is the centralized banking system of the United States. The federal government controls communications through the Federal Communications Commission and transportation through the Department of Transportation. *Common Core* and the public school system is a dream come true for Marxist ideology.

"When government fears the people, there is liberty. When the people fear the government, there is tyranny."

—Thomas Jefferson

Do you fear the government? According to The Heritage Foundation, our Congress has written over 4,500 criminal offenses into federal statutes. Worse yet, unelected bureaucrats have instituted over 300,000 regulations that subject the American people to criminal prosecution.[16] It has been reported that the average U.S. citizen commits three felony violations per day. That is not freedom. There is a reason that most law-abiding citizens fear the government. Most citizens do not have the financial means to fight a government that has the unlimited power and resources to charge, try, and convict. This

---

[16] Paul Rosenzweig, "Ignorance of the Law is No Excuse, But It Is Reality," *The Heritage Foundation* June 17, 2013, http://www.heritage.org/research/reports/2013/06/ignorance-of-the-law-is-no-excuse-but-it-is-reality.

is in direct opposition to the ideals and goals the founders of our nation were striving to establish when they wrote a Constitution that put the power in the hands of the people and not the government.

We would do well to take a serious look at the "Bill of Rights" and consider where we are today as a nation. The First Amendment to the Constitution guarantees five freedoms: freedom of religion, freedom of speech, freedom of the press, the right to peacefully assemble, and the right to petition the government for redress of grievances.

In the previous chapter we addressed the attack on freedom of religion. Do you feel confident in the freedom of speech, press, peaceful assembly, or your ability to redress the government?

The Second Amendment states, *"The right of the people to keep and bear arms, shall not be infringed."* We see that the right of people to keep and bear arms is restricted in many places across the country, yet the Constitution states it shall not be infringed. The reason the founders wanted to avoid infringement against that right was not for hunting or sport shooting, but to protect the people against a tyrannical government.

The Fourth Amendment: our right to privacy. "*The right of the people to be secure in their persons, houses, papers and effects against unreasonable searches and seizures, shall not be violated, and no Warrants shall be issued but upon probable cause...*" Your privacy is being violated every day with the government collecting and storing every phone call, text, and email.

The Fifth Amendment protects your rights against double jeopardy, self-incrimination, and deprivation of life, liberty, or property without the due process of law. It also ensures that your property will not be taken for public use without just compensation. Double jeopardy seems to be intact, but how about self-incrimination? If the government is collecting everything you are saying and writing, then they are violating your protection against becoming a witness against yourself. We will address the confiscation of private property later.

The Tenth Amendment states that the powers not given to the United States by the Constitution are reserved to the states or to the people. To reiterate, the Constitution only gave the federal government eighteen specifically defined and limited powers. Today, we see an out-of-control federal government with seemingly unlimited power, and even worse, we see state governments becoming no more than conduits of destructive federal policy imposed by threat, coercion, or extortion.

Private property ownership was undoubtedly considered one of the most critical elements of freedom; without the ability to own private property there was no freedom. Do you own private property? If you do, then stop paying taxes on it. Before long, you will get a notice that the state is going to confiscate your property. Can you leave your land to your children without the government taking a portion of it or taxing them heavily? Private property tax is nothing more than an effective tool for government to abolish private property ownership. Today, you rent property from the government rather than own it. Income tax is the close relative of property tax. You labor for pay, your wages become your property; the government confiscates a portion of your labor for itself and cedes the remainder to you.

Furthermore, regarding taxation, the founders were quite blunt on their assessment of taxation at the federal level—none. They believed that charity began in the home and extended to the community. They gave the states the right to tax but felt that it was immoral to take money from working people to give to the town drunk so he could spend his nights in the tavern and days sleeping on the park bench. Government taxation has become nothing more than a powerful tool in which the government can legally acquire the property of its citizens.

Popular thought is that the Revolutionary War was brought about primarily because of taxation, and although taxation was an issue, it was number 17 out of 27 issues they cited with the British Crown in the Declaration of Independence. Frederic Bastiat in *The Law* describes taxation as "legalized plunder." He explains property and plunder in this manner:

> *Man can live and satisfy his wants only by ceaseless labor; by the ceaseless application of his faculties to natural resources. This process is the origin of property. But it is also true that a man may live and satisfy his wants by seizing and consuming the products of the labor of others. This process is the origin of plunder. Now since man is naturally inclined to avoid pain—and since labor is pain in itself—it follows that men will resort to*

plunder whenever plunder is easier than work.[17]

Welfare, food stamps, and universal health care are forms of legalized plunder because Congress has passed laws that allow one citizen to take the fruit of another citizen's labor without committing a crime.

Legalized plunder has its roots in socialism and communism. Frederic Bastiat, in *The Law*, also said, "**Legal plunder has two roots: One of them, as I have said before, is in human greed; the other is in false philanthropy.**"[18] He explains that "false philanthropy" is the work of legislators. Legislators, through legislation, basically take what is not theirs and give to those who have not earned it. In the end, those in the government are thought to be the compassionate, giving individuals. Of course, some do it out of compassion, while most do it to be re-elected by those who are receiving welfare, food stamps, and universal health care—at the expense of those who continue to be productive citizens. In truth, using the law to "spread the wealth" is not social justice, but injustice imposed on a population. One sector has their livelihood plundered; the

---

[17] Frederic Bastiat, *The Law*, trans. Dean Russel (New York: Foundation for Economic Education, 2007), 5.
[18] Bastiat, *The Law,* 17.

other sector becomes enslaved to the government through handouts.

Today, we have a national debt of over $18 trillion and a Congress unwilling to address the crisis in any meaningful way. They continue to raise the debt limit without any attempt to cut worthless and failed government programs. Their only solution to fixing failing government programs is to push more tax dollars and government employees at the problem.

Let us examine money issued by the Federal Reserve, which is a private banking cartel, not a federal government entity. This private organization controls the nation's money supply. As someone once said, "The Federal Reserve is as federal as Federal Express." This money is known as fiat currency because it is not tied to gold or silver and, therefore, has no intrinsic value. <u>Every country since the Roman Empire that issued fiat currency has collapsed</u>. The value of the dollar is solely based on the good name of the United States. The government has been counterfeiting our currency since it went off the gold standard in 1971.

The perfect storm is brewing—fiat currency, national debt, and monetizing debt by printing money to pay the debt—all these have caused the United States' reputation as a nation of integrity to be tarnished. The dollar has lost its AAA rating, and countries around the world are looking for a new world reserve currency. Unless we see a drastic change in monetary policy within our country, it is guaranteed that our economy will collapse.

We hear about the failing social security system and its inability to meet the needs of our senior citizens, while the federal government spends over $100 billion a year to feed, house, educate, and medicate illegal aliens.

Congress passed *The Immigration Act of 1891* as a result of millions of immigrants entering the United States. It was passed to exclude some immigrants from admission to the United States. Those excluded included, *"All idiots, insane persons, pauper or persons likely to become a public charge, persons suffering from a loathsome or a dangerous contagious disease, persons who have been convicted of a felony or other infamous crime or misdemeanor involving moral turpitude, polygamists..."* [19] In March 2015, Immigration and Customs Enforcement announced it had released another 30,000 criminal aliens into the population during 2014. That brings the total to 167,000 non-detained

---

[19] FIFTY-FIRST CONGRESS. Sess. II. CH. 550,551. 1891.

criminal aliens roaming America's streets.[20] Immigration control was a means of protecting the nation and its citizens; today it is not even a consideration of the government.

At what point does illegal immigration become an invasion? A report from the *Center for Immigration Studies* reports that we will have 51 million immigrants in eight years.[21] We have a Congress that refuses to do its job in securing our borders, but is most willing to engage in extra-Constitutional activities daily.

The state of our nation today is a result of not enough citizens understanding the Constitution and the limits imposed on the federal government by that Constitution. As the electorate, our silence has enabled the federal government to enact legislation which has restricted—and will become more restrictive—of your God-given rights to life, liberty, and private property. The good news is: YOU can fix it! All you have to do is become well-educated regarding our Constitution. The

---

[20] Chris Chmielenski, "Obama Admin. Releases another 30,000 criminal aliens; 167 non-detained criminal aliens on U.S. streets," *NumbersUSA* March 20, 2015.

[21] Paul Bedard, "Census: Record 51 million immigrants in 8 years, will account for 82% of U.S. growth," *Washington Examiner* April 22, 2015, http://www.washingtonexaminer.com/census-record-51-million-immigrants-in-8-years-will-account-for-82-of-u.s.-growth/article/2563463

Constitution, our rule of law, is the only defense you and every other citizen have against the out-of-control federal government that is in power today. John Jay, the first Chief Justice of the Supreme Court, said, "*Every member of the State ought diligently to read and to study the constitution and teach the rising generation to be free. By knowing their rights, they will sooner perceive when they are violated, and be the better prepared to defend and assert them.*" It is time for you to know and understand your rights and begin to assert them.

The Spirit of Party

"However combinations or associations of the above description may now and then answer popular ends, they are likely, in the course of time and things, to become potent engines, by which cunning, ambitious, and unprincipled men will be enabled to subvert the power of the people and to usurp for themselves the reins of government, destroying afterwards the very engines which have lifted them to their unjust dominion."

—George Washington, Farewell Address to Congress

The American ideals of life, liberty, and private property have been usurped by the insatiable greed of the two-party system for wealth and power. The common bond, our Constitution, which once made the nation prosperous with liberty and justice for all, has been continually ignored by the Democrat and Republican parties. Political parties are wholly responsible for the destruction of the principles that once made the United States unique among nations.

Today, the Republican and Democrat parties have a stranglehold on the future of our nation. They have engaged in the deadly suppression of our Constitution, which will result in an inevitable death spiral toward the abyss. George Washington, in his farewell address to Congress over 200 years ago, warned us about the "spirit of party" which we observe flourishing without restraint in our nation. We see it in the epic battles that are being waged between citizens of our country who have pledged their loyalty to either the Democrat or Republican parties rather than the nation. It is important to note that the two-party system is not mentioned or sanctioned in the Constitution. The Democrat and Republican parties are private organizations that have taken over the power of our government and subverted the power of the people.

George Washington continued in his farewell address to further describe the "spirit of party":

The alternate domination of one faction over another, sharpened by the spirit of revenge, natural to party dissension, which in different ages and countries has perpetrated the most horrid enormities, is itself a frightful despotism. But this leads at length to a more formal and permanent despotism. The disorders and miseries which result gradually incline the minds of men to seek security and repose in the absolute power of an individual; and sooner or later the chief of some prevailing faction, more able or more fortunate than his competitors, turns this disposition to the purposes of his own elevation, on the ruins of public liberty.

Without looking forward to an extremity of this kind (which nevertheless ought not to be entirely out of sight), <u>the common and continual mischiefs of the spirit of party are sufficient to make it the interest and duty of a wise people to discourage and restrain it.</u>

It serves always to distract the public councils and enfeeble the public administration. It agitates the community with ill-founded jealousies and false alarms, kindles the animosity of one part against another, *foments occasionally riot and insurrection. It opens the door to foreign influence and corruption, which finds a facilitated access to the government itself through the channels of party passions...* [underlining added]

Can we find a more accurate description of where we find the government of the United States today? George Washington tried to warn us of the destructive power of political parties whose lust for power would usurp the power of the people and end with the very destruction of our liberty. He told us that it was the responsibility of a wise people to discourage and restrain the parties. We have failed to heed his prophetic insight, and it has resulted in a dysfunctional government without the will or desire to cede power back to the states and the people.

What George Washington did not envision was that the political parties, left unchecked, would eventually evolve into singularity. Singularity is the state, fact, quality, or condition of being singular. Today, at the top of the political parties, they have reached singularity in their destruction of the American Constitution. This is not to say that there are not individuals who take their oath seriously; it is, however, to say that the party elite and leadership simply silence their voice.

The 2014 elections indicated an overwhelming desire of the American people to change the direction of our country. The Republican Party promised a halt to illegal immigration and the end of universal health care. However, instead of honoring their promises to the electorate, we see the same policies being fully supported by party leadership on both sides of the aisle.

The political parties have no more concern for the future of the people or our nation than two rival gangs. They both want to maintain their market share of power, influence, and wealth without a concern for the inevitable outcome of their irresponsible behavior. They inflame the passions of men with rhetoric while on the campaign trail, only to find full agreement in the halls of Congress. They artfully use fear, intimidation, and favor to control the population and effectively pit one segment of the population against the other.

One of the biggest lies perpetrated on the American people is that fault for all evils that assail the nation is the responsibility of a sitting President. We have three branches of government, each given different powers to provide checks and balances, to ensure that no one branch can exercise complete power of the government. This is known as the separation of powers. Another lie taught in schools is that the branches are co-equal in power. The Constitution gives more power to one branch—Congress. The founders understood that in the representative republic, the branch closest to the people needed to maintain the most power. The founders intended that the people would be the arbitrators of a just government and fully empowered to replace failing members of Congress by voting in free elections—every two years for the House of Representatives and every six years for the Senate.

Congress thrives on opposition Presidents. The President becomes the scapegoat for every failing government policy and ensures job security during the next election cycle. Because the people are largely ignorant of the Constitution and the functions of government, Congress is seldom held accountable for their failure to "support and defend the Constitution" and can effectively conceal their cowardly and unethical behavior by blaming their inactivity on another branch of government.

Perhaps you believe there is a difference between the parties. You may be thinking one is liberal and one is conservative. I maintain that is in rhetoric only. Give some thought to the following questions and ask yourself how the political parties differ in policies that are destroying our country.

Which party has increased taxes? Which party has increased the size of government? Which party has increased the number of regulations? Which party supports illegal immigration? Which party supports the continued empowerment of the NSA and IRS?

Voting in Congress and the Senate is largely a political shell game. Politicians vote <u>for</u> bills—and then <u>against</u> them—when they are high on the public's radar. The parties determine how many votes they need to pass a bill, and then give representatives the ability to opt out if it is sensitive in their district. This becomes powerful re-election campaign fodder for the public. Unless you follow the bills closely, you will never know if they supported or defended your position. There should only be three criteria for voting in favor of a bill:

1. Is it Constitutional?
2. Do we need it?
3. Can we afford it?

If it doesn't satisfy those three criteria, the elected members of both houses of Congress have an obligation to vote against it; otherwise, they are violating their oath to the Constitution, and to you. It's certainly not the duty of elected representatives or political parties to vote largess and use the treasury to buy votes, nor to vote for feel-good legislation that violates the Constitution.

Ballot access is the most potent engine for maintaining control of the election process and ensuring the monopoly of the Democrat and Republican parties. As long as these two private organizations, the Democrat and Republican parties, maintain power over the ballot, they will maintain power over the government.

Recently, there has been much ado about creating closed primaries in the state of Montana and how that will install integrity into the ballot process. I received a letter from a friend and former Montana legislator, Rick Jore, who fully understands the heart of this matter, which directly affects the future of our nation. I have reprinted portions of his letter with his permission:

September 18, 2014

...Political parties are private organizations. Why are the taxpayers funding what should be the private business of these private organizations, that of nominating which candidates should represent them in the general

election? Not only are these private organizations being subsidized via primary elections, they are being subsidized to the exclusion of all other private organizations.

Many groups and organizations have a keen interest in electing their chosen candidate to public office. Why is it that only political parties get a subsidized nomination process and a label on the general election ballot? How in the world can we justify what amounts to taxpayer subsidized advertising for political parties...and this to the exclusion of all other private organizations?

These two things—tax funded primaries and party labels on the ballot—have created a ballot access monopoly for political parties that can gain ballot access status, which invariably will "weed out" all but two. Where in the state or federal constitution is there any hint about a "two party system"? (Ironically, for all intents and purposes, "open primaries" make this "two party system" a de facto "one party system.")

The Montana Constitution establishes qualifications for public office. Every qualified citizen should have opportunity to file and campaign for public office. They should have that opportunity equally with all other qualified candidates, including being listed on the ballot with no label behind their name. That right has been taken away in all statewide races and most local races, thanks to the ballot monopoly of two parties.

Instead of enacting "additional qualifications" as allowed for in the Montana Constitution (Article IV Sec. 4), the legislature has actually enacted restrictions for anyone who does not file as a member of a qualified political party to be on the ballot. (For example, getting a certain number of signatures to be on the ballot has nothing to do with "qualifications." It has everything to do with "a requirement" and "a restriction." Even then, one must still have a label, even if an (I), behind his name.)

There is nothing wrong with political parties or party membership. There is something wrong with giving them tax subsidies to control the ballot.

My conclusion? Do away with tax funded "primaries" altogether. Remove party labels from the ballot. Level the "playing field" for all qualified candidates per the constitution. If there is concern about winning candidates not getting a plurality of votes in the general election, have a runoff of the top two vote-getters only in those races where one candidate did not get that plurality. This would be no more expensive than the two elections taxpayers are now funding...and it would restore and maintain the integrity of our election process.

Rick Jore

Ronan, MT

The Democrat and Republican parties have waged a successful insurgency against the American people by systematically undermining the Constitution. We have allowed cunning, ambitious, unprincipled men to take the power from the people and seize the reins of our government. The titles Democrat and Republican are simply a distinction without a difference.

Article 1, Section 9, of the Constitution states: "*No Title of Nobility shall be granted by the United States: and no Person holding any Office of Profit or Trust under them, shall, without the Consent of the Congress, accept of any present, Emolument, Office, or Title, of any kind whatever, from any King, Prince, or foreign State.*" We have unwittingly transformed our elected officials into the New Aristocracy, complete with titles of Congressman, Senator, Supreme Court Judge, and President—the ruling class answerable only to the party and not the people.

The Democrat and Republican parties have stolen our birthright of freedom and prosperity. We have willingly followed and supported those who have violated the law and promised peace and security, and we now know we have neither. They have no power we haven't given them, and we are the only ones who can take it away. We have faithfully supported the parties with our money, our time, our voice, and our vote. We have empowered them to take away our life, our liberty, and our personal property. We have traded freedom and opportunity for bread and circuses.

Each of us is the key to effectively destroy this insurgency known as the Democrat and Republican parties. If we take no action, they will surely destroy our nation. It is time to follow sound biblical advice: *"But find some capable, honest men who fear God and hate bribes. Appoint them as judges over groups of one thousand, one hundred, fifty, and ten."*— Exodus 18:21. We need representatives who fear God and understand our Constitution. It is time to hold all elected officials responsible for their violations of the Constitution and ensure they are never again empowered to take our God-given rights. Time is of the essence; we must restore the proper functions of government. <u>It is time for you to throw away party titles and simply become an "American."</u>

A House Divided

"Every kingdom divided against itself is brought to desolation, and every city or house divided against itself will not stand."

—Matthew 12:25

Economic disaster, repressive governments, and religious persecution brought millions of immigrants to the shores of the United States. They came from every nation, speaking different languages, and with vastly different cultural backgrounds to become Americans. They came with nothing more than hope for an opportunity to build a better future for themselves and their families, not for a hand out.

The United States became known as "the melting pot." The motto of the United States is "*E Pluribus Unum*"—out of many, one. The desire was one nation under God, where all men are treated equally and with justice for all.

The United States has been described as something quite different today. We used to be a "melting pot," where everyone believed in the dream of the United States and found pride in being an American. It is now being described as a "salad bowl." If you are a tomato, you are never lettuce; if you are a carrot, you are never a cucumber. Immigrants are trying to avoid assimilating. They want the American language, culture, and religion to become subservient to the despotism from which they escaped.

The federal government has run an effective campaign of "*divide and conquer*" in the last few decades. Our government has systematically driven a wedge between every man, woman, and child. It is no longer good enough to be an American. People who have never been to Africa are African-Americans, and we have Mexican-Americans, Asian-Americans, and Native Americans. The United States was never a place where you lost your identity or culture, nor was it was a place where your culture was given legal status or supremacy over American culture. We have lost the ideal of what it means to be an American; no longer out of many, one—now it is out of many, many. Every man, woman and child is divided into categories of the smallest detail. You are divided by race, religion, age, gender, and sexual orientation.

In the first place we should insist that the immigrant who comes here in good faith becomes an American and assimilates himself to us, he shall be treated on an exact equity with everyone else, for it is an outrage to discriminate against any such man because of a creed, or birthplace or origin. But this is predicated upon the man's becoming an American and nothing but an American. We have room for but one flag, the American flag . . . We have room for but one language here, and that is the English language . . . and we have room for but one sole loyalty and that is a loyalty to the American people.

—Theodore Roosevelt

Revisionist history has become an art in our public school system. Heroes of the past have become the villains of today. The focus has become the failings of our nation and not how the country overcame those failings. Children are now programmed to have an attitude of resentment towards American culture and society, or equipped with an excuse for failure, based on how their ancestors were treated. Children are taught to become victims rather than victors.

The government has become the single biggest purveyor and promoter of discord and division in the nation. They no longer promote American values or American exceptionalism, but proclaim how unjust the United States has been in the treatment of other nations. Politicians have weaponized class warfare in our nation as an effective means to gain votes. They tout social justice as a means to acquire something an individual has not earned. If an individual does not acquire fame or fortune, it is because he or she was discriminated against or there was a "glass ceiling" preventing their rise to stardom. In actuality, more people fail for lack of healthy work ethic or because of a poor attitude.

Article 1, Section 2, of the Constitution establishes that the government would conduct a census every ten years. This enumeration of the population was to establish the number of representatives each state would have in Congress. The census today, however, has become an effective tool for gathering vast amounts of personal or private information. Census takers now ask about: your income, employment, if you have a flush-toilet, the time you leave for work, if you have serious difficulty in concentrating, remembering, or making decisions because of a physical, mental, or emotional condition—to cite a few examples of their questions. Every conceivable opportunity to classify people as different from one another, under the guise of data collection, is exercised by a government that was set up for three things: to protect your life, liberty, and property. You have to wonder what the reason is behind collecting all this data. Is it simply to justify the existence of a government program, to increase government funding for failed projects, or is it something more nefarious?

America has always been a nation of diversity. The founding fathers came from different political, cultural, and religious backgrounds. They were in sharp disagreement over almost everything, save the creation of our nation. They knew when to lay aside differences for the preservation of the greatest opportunity men might ever have to live free.

Europe is decades ahead of the United States in another great divider known as multiculturalism. Unless we learn from the mistakes of European nations, we are destined to repeat them and experience the same problems in our country. European leaders like German Chancellor Merkel, British Prime Minister Cameron, and former French President Sarkozy have all publicly stated that multiculturalism is a failure. Multiculturalism has not worked anywhere and will not work in the United States. Yet, we see the rise of sharia law within the

United States in states with large Muslim communities. Honor killings, child brides, polygamy, women and children being treated like chattel, female genital mutilation, and slavery have no place in American culture and no part in a free country.

"One country, one constitution, one destiny."
—Daniel Webster

As a nation, the United States has spent unknown fortunes creating the world's best military to defend our nation. Hundreds of thousands of lives have been lost and fortunes spent to bring freedom to the oppressed around the world. Our strength has always been in our unity—one vision of liberty and justice for all. Those who want to destroy our culture, values, and future understand our nation will not fail or fall because our military is not strong enough. They know that they can only destroy it from within. We can no longer allow diversity and multiculturalism to be used as tools to destroy private businesses or burn cities.

The only social justice we will ever see is when we learn to "love our neighbor as we love ourselves." Every attempt by the government to legislate justice ensures that someone will lose freedom.

"Remember upon the conduct of each depends the fate of all."

—Alexander The Great

Two of the most divisive and distrusted titles used in America today are Republican and Democrat. They are closely followed by two of the most ill-defined and antagonistic words used in the American lexicon: liberal and conservative. Citizens line up on opposing sides in the same manner as sports fans chanting sophomoric, illogical mantras hoping that their political team will win the national championship, even as they are tearing the national fabric to shreds. They are used like sports team logos to unite opposing forces for national sports titles, while the real game being played on the international stage—the survival of team USA—is in certain peril.

Man or woman, white or black, young or old—you are the only one who can bring unity to the nation. It takes love of God, man, and country to lay aside those issues that divide us and focus on the principles that unite us. It takes courage, not compromise, to speak the truth and oppose those forces that would divide us.

The time to do nothing has passed; you can no longer hide in the crowd or wait for the next George Washington to lead you. Our country will surely disintegrate if you remain silent and inactive. There is only you, self-government, the strongest most powerful government in the world, standing between destruction and restoration of our nation.

Globalism

"To achieve world government, it is necessary to remove from the minds of men their individualism, loyalty to family traditions, national patriotism, and religious dogmas."
—Brock Adams, Director UN Health Organization

In his farewell address to congress, George Washington went into great detail to warn of the danger of entanglements with foreign nations:

> *The great rule of conduct for us in regard to foreign nations is in extending our commercial relations, to have with them as little political connection as possible. So far as we have already formed engagements, let them be fulfilled with perfect good faith. Here let us stop . . . It is our true policy to*

steer clear of permanent alliances with any
portion of the foreign world...

Thomas Jefferson said in his first Inaugural Address: "*...peace, commerce, and honest friendship with all nations, entangling alliances with none...*"

The founders were not isolationists; they were separatists who believed we should avoid foreign entanglements that compromised the sovereignty of the nation. Today, as a nation, we find ourselves entangled in a world government organization made up of 193 nation states, the United Nations. The majority of these nations have little in common with the principles that made the United States the freest, most prosperous nation in the world. These nations are ruled by monarchs, dictators, or oligarchies—in direct contrast to our representative republic.

Following the "war to end all wars," WWI, came the *Treaty of Versailles*. President Wilson travelled to Paris to present his 14 points; the final point was the creation of the League of Nations. He wanted to create a new world order designed to maintain world peace. When he returned to the United States, he attempted to get the Senate to ratify the treaty so the United States could become part of the League of Nations. He failed. Senators believed that the collective security agreement would sacrifice national sovereignty. This was the first attempt to bring the United States into a world government body.

Prior to the close of WWII, in January 1943, Secretary of State Cordell Hull and five others drafted the original proposal for the United Nations. They presented it to President Roosevelt in June 1944, and held the founding conference in San Francisco in 1945. The Secretary-General of the conference was the infamous Alger Hiss, who was later convicted of being a Soviet spy. The Senate ratified the document and ushered the United States into world government. With an $8.5 million donation from John D. Rockefeller, Jr., land was purchased in New York for its headquarters.[22]

The UN has done little to bring peace and prosperity to the world. Equality and justice—unalienable rights given by God and maintained by government—are indeed foreign concepts in most of the member nations, yet we find ourselves entangled in their oppressive attempts to control. UN governorship writes rules and regulations that are specifically designed to circumvent the sovereignty of the United States and all nation states, making

---

[22] James Perloff, *The Shadows of Power The Council on Foreign Relations And The American Decline*, (Appleton, Wisconsin: Western Islands Publishers, 1988) 71.

nations subservient to a global ruling body. These rules and regulations specifically violate our God-given rights to life, liberty, and private property ownership.

UN Earth Summit Agenda 21

The most powerful attack on life, liberty, and property ownership can be found in the *UN Earth Summit Agenda 21*, originally signed by President George H. Bush in 1992. When I first heard of *Agenda 21*, I reasoned that the person telling me about it was some lost soul, delusional with conspiracy theories. As a former intelligence officer, I took the challenge and researched it for myself. What I found out was vastly more disturbing than I could have imagined. *Agenda 21* has been supported by Republican and Democrat presidents since 1992, and has enormous overreach into the lives of every American citizen.

Subsequent Presidential actions have strengthened *Agenda 21*'s "Sustainable Development" policies in the United States. Executive actions have opened a pathway for globalist agendas to introduce and legislate *Agenda 21* policies at local, state, and national levels. A cursory investigation into the widespread use of "Sustainable Development" in government regulation will show how powerful and well established this international, foreign law has become in the fabric of our nation.

Make no mistake—*Agenda 21* is about global control and the abolishment of individual rights. It is centered on environmental policies designed to restrict individual rights, freedoms, and choice. The primary source document used to give you a synopsis for *Agenda 21* is the UN's own *Earth Summit Agenda 21* publication. This document is formulated around the idea of redistribution of wealth from developed nations to developing nations. Success rests on the UN's ability to restrict the liberties and resources of the populations of developed nations like the United States.

The Secretary General of the *UN's 1992 Earth Summit*, Maurice Strong, outlined the complete agenda with the following statement: *"Current lifestyles and consumption patterns of the affluent middle class—involving high meat intake, use of fossil fuels, appliances, home and work air conditioning, and suburban housing—are not sustainable."*[23] The world's affluent middle class represents much of the population of the United States. The UN wants to control what

---

[23] Christian Gomez, "Agenda 21 And You," (Appleton, WI: The John Birch Society, 2011) 2.

you eat, what you drive, the appliances you use, the temperature of your home and office, and ultimately where you live. Never do the elite and globalists address their own lifestyles. Their hypocritical condemnation of the use of natural resources, environmental scare tactics, and need to sacrifice for the poor are always aimed at the population they want to control, while never intending to change a scintilla of their extravagant lifestyles.

For ease of digestion, I will briefly outline a few of the chapters of the *Earth Summit Agenda 21* publication, which is the hallmark document used by the global elite to invade every facet of your life. I encourage you to do your own research. I have found that many citizens in the United States are unaware of this far-reaching agenda designed to control your future.

Chapter 1 is the preamble, so we will begin with Chapter 2: "International Cooperation to Accelerate Sustainable Development in Developing Countries and Related Domestic Policies." This chapter tells how the UN plans to control food production and economic justice for developing countries by *"promoting sustainable development through international trade agreements."* They want to manipulate international production and consumption through trade agreements controlled by the UN. Since they believe that *"the commodity* sector dominates the economies of many developing countries," the UN wants to remove all trade barriers. They propose a system of social justice by controlling production in affluent countries, while removing any national trade barriers that would protect U.S. farmers, ranchers, miners, loggers, industry, and all other productive American industries.

The UN wants to control global trade, which is stated as follows: "*Trade liberalization should therefore be pursued on a global basis across economic sectors so as to contribute to sustainable development.*" This is simply a policy of leveling the playing field for third world countries specifically designed to penalize developed countries. In other words, collective farming and industrial production failed in Russia, yet the UN wants to institute them on a global scale. They would like to facilitate this through the International Monetary Fund (IMF) and the World Bank.

Chapter 3 deals with combatting poverty. Who among us would not like to see the elimination of poverty? Although a noble gesture that plucks at our heartstrings, the reality is that poverty will never be eliminated. The affluent, global elitists talk about greater equity in income distribution, with their main focus, as Maurice Strong said, "the affluent middle class" of the world.

This chapter has much to do with the obvious ways to lift the poor through education and opportunity. Interestingly, though, it also subtly introduces population control mechanisms through empowering women, health care access, and education in order to match resources with population.

Chapter 4 deals with "Changing Consumption Patterns." The UN wants to focus on "unsustainable patterns of production and consumption." They propose that poverty stems from environmental degradation. They put forth that "...*the major cause of the continued deterioration of the global environment is the unsustainable pattern of consumption and production, particularly in industrialized countries, which is a matter of grave concern, aggravating poverty and imbalances.*" The UN is gravely concerned about the amount of production and consumption in developed countries. The UN maintains that the U.S. consumes and produces too much, which is harmful to the environment. The UN believes that if they can reduce the U.S. to a third world status, then they can save the planet.

This chapter defies logic; developed nations are far more protective of the environment than developing nations. In earlier chapters, the UN wants to open trade for agriculture and industry products to pass unhindered from third world nations into nations like the United States. Now, they say that developed nations need to reduce industry and agriculture (production and consumption). Is this so that developed, environmentally sound nations can become dependent on unproductive, environmentally unsound, developing nations?

Here is how the UN openly condemns the lifestyles you and I live: "*Although consumption patterns are very high in certain parts of the world, the basic consumer needs of a large section of humanity are not being met. This results in excessive demands and unsustainable lifestyles among the richer segments, which place immense stress on the environment.*" They go on to say that developed nations, like the U.S., "*should take the lead in achieving sustainable consumption patterns.*" I fail to see how the corresponding action of the reduction of waste, production, and consumption in the United States will transcend to an affluent middle class in Africa. In the history of man taking from one and giving to another, poverty has never been eliminated.

Chapter 5 is titled: "Demographic Dynamics and Sustainability"; it focuses on the more basic ideals of globalists who have an unnatural fear of overpopulation. As stated, "...*the growth of world population and production, combined with unsustainable consumption patterns, places increasingly severe stress on the life-supporting capacities of our planet. These interactive processes affect the use of land, water, air, energy, and other resources.*" Their solution for all concerned is population control. It centers on "...*improving the status of women and demographic dynamics, particularly through women's access to education, primary and reproductive health care programmes, economic independence and their effective, equitable participation in all levels of decision-making.*" Their belief includes insistence that through abortion we can save the planet for the select few. We need only to eliminate the unworthy consumers in order to preserve resources for the worthy.

For brevity, I will bypass Chapter 6 on health issues, and skip to Chapter 7: "Promoting Sustainable Human Settlement Development." The idea here is that people have so mismanaged land and resources that we need to remove them from the land and resettle them in population centers. This is a basic plan to depopulate rural areas and establish forbidden zones in order to protect the environment from people.

The global agenda is to establish resettlement areas to house the masses, control their reproduction, consumption of goods, access to land, and need to travel with resultant complete dependence on international law and government for survival. See *Agenda 21* map below:

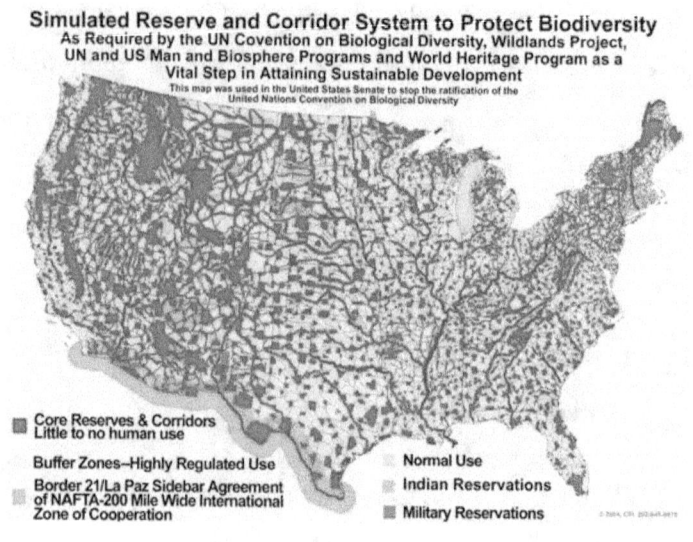

Simulated Reserve and Corridor System to Protect Biodiversity
As Required by the UN Convention on Biological Diversity, Wildlands Project, UN and US Man and Biosphere Programs and World Heritage Program as a Vital Step in Attaining Sustainable Development
This map was used in the United States Senate to stop the ratification of the United Nations Convention on Biological Diversity

Core Reserves & Corridors
Little to no human use

Buffer Zones–Highly Regulated Use

Border 21/La Paz Sidebar Agreement of NAFTA-200 Mile Wide International Zone of Cooperation

Normal Use

Indian Reservations

Military Reservations

Chapter 8 deals with developing an integrated legal and regulatory framework of establishing governing laws to protect the environment. To sum it up, in their own words: *"The responsibility for bringing about changes lies with Governments in partnership with the private sector and local authorities, and in collaboration with national, regional and international organizations, including, in particular, UNEP, UNDP and the World Bank."* The UN envisions member nations passing laws and regulations to support its radical environmental policies. It would also like to leverage the World Bank to ensure compliance. In the U.S. we can already see the explosion of environmental law that puts more government control over air, land, and water.

There are 23 more chapters dealing with a litany of additional restrictions on your freedom: from non-motorized transportation to strengthening the role of workers and their trade unions. This is, bar none, one of the most anti-American, anti-freedom documents designed by man. It is all encompassing and ultimately designed to control all activities of man through global government. I encourage you to research for yourself the points I have addressed, and I am trusting that you will realize the urgency of action to restore our sovereignty.

Implementation of UN Policies

So how do these UN policies get implemented in a free country? One approach is through the executive branch of government. President Obama will use "Obamatrade" as a tool to solve climate change. [24] The White House released an announcement on a climate change agreement with China on November 11, 2014, which stated, *"The United States intends to achieve an economy-wide target of reducing its emissions by 26-28% below its 2005 level in 2025..."*[25] It further stated that China only had to reduce its emissions by 20% by 2030. It does not take much analysis to see that de-industrialization policies in the U.S. economy support UN *Agenda 21.* Through both trade agreements and executive action, facilitated by extremist environmental agendas and fueled by international consensus, the devastating impact on all forms of production in the U.S. is inevitable. Think about how the government will mandate CO_2 emission reduction of 28 percent from cars, trucks, manufacturing, and farming. Who will pay the cost? Certainly not a bankrupt federal government; the American taxpayer will be forced to do so.

---

[24] Howard Richman, "Obama admits that climate change will be in Obamatrade,"*American Thinker* June 4 2015, http://www.americanthinker.com/blog/2015/06/obama_admits_that_climate_change_will_be_in_obamatrade.html.
[25] The White House Office of the Press Secretary, "U.S.-China Joint Announcement on Climate Change," *The White House* Nov 11 2014, https://www.whitehouse.gov/the-press-office/2014/11/11/us-china-joint-announcement-climate-change

Search for "sustainability" in your community and see what you come up with. The UN implements many of the *Agenda 21* policies through its *International Council for Local Environmental Initiatives* (ICLEI) offices. The ICLEI USA website boasts of having *"in the United States, 450 member cities and counties including small rural towns and bustling metropolises in 46 states."* Go to www.icleiusa.org to find out if there is an ICLEI office near you. You will be surprised at the influence they have had in your community—developing green space, bike paths and other sustainable development projects.

There was indeed a time when individuals and corporations polluted our air, land, and water without restriction. Many had little or no concern for the destruction they caused, and we have all benefited from regulation and education that has preserved the health of both people and the environment. However, we have quickly passed from no regulation to over-regulation, to the detriment of our future, freedom, and prosperity. Environmentalism has become a weaponized tool in the hands of government to restrict life, liberty, and private property ownership. To put things into perspective, recently the President signed an executive order, *"Planning for Federal*

Sustainability in the next Decade."[26] "***On May 27, 2015,
President Obama signed a new regulation giving the EPA
regulatory authority and government dominion over streams,
creeks, brooks, rivulets, burns, tributaries, wetlands—even
ditches and possibly, really big puddles.***'[27] This could quite
possibly be the biggest land grab of private property in the
history of our nation.

It defies all reason that the citizens of the United States
would cede their lives, liberty, and property to the UN. There are
few member nations in the UN who have anything in common
with the United States. Most are led by monarchs, dictators, or
oligarchies. They differ drastically in culture, religion, and
wealth; and they want to change all three in the United States.
The only ones standing between global government, UN *Agenda
21*, and the sovereignty of the United States are you and other
like-minded Americans. The UN is a corrupt governing body
without the financial resources or military to enforce their global
agenda without the consent of member nations. It is time to
elect representatives who believe in the sovereignty of the United

---

[26] Barack Obama. "Planning for Federal Sustainability in the Next
Decade," Executive Order 13693, March 19, 2015.
[27] Joseph Curl, "Democrats Join GOP to Fight Obama Admin's New
Rule on Streams, Creeks," *Washington Times*, (Washington, D.C.), May
28, 2015.

States and refuse to bend the knee to the oppressive dictates of this incompetent world body.

In many states, citizens have started to recognize the danger of these radical environmental agendas designed to control their lives. Develop and nurture an alliance with your city council members, county commissioners, state representatives, and all those who oppose the introduction of foreign laws into your courts. If that is not possible, I urge you to investigate and educate yourself, your family, and friends, and then stand against this radical world agenda.

Centralization

*"The central bank is an institution of the
most deadly hostility existing against the
Principles and form of our Constitution. I am
an Enemy to all banks discounting bills or
notes for anything but Coin. If the American
People allow private banks to control the
issuance of their currency, first by inflation
and then by deflation, the banks and
corporations that will grow up around them
will deprive the People of all their Property
until their Children will wake up homeless on
the continent their Fathers conquered."*
—Thomas Jefferson

Once banks go negative on interest rates, depositors will
start removing their assets from the banks. The only way to
ensure everyone is taxed for having money in the bank is to move

the banking system to a cashless digital system. What will be the next big crisis in the United States that will persuade you to give away more of your freedom for a false sense of security?

The next major crisis might not be a terrorist attack, but rather the Federal Reserve convincing the government to move to a cashless society so that physical currency is outlawed, whereupon all will have to transition to digital currency for the survival of our economy. This would empower the central banks to move to negative interest rates on all private and business accounts, essentially taxing any currency assets you store in a bank.

Some recent headlines:

"United States government is $18 trillion in debt..."

"G-20 conference votes for bail-in program allowing banks to confiscate depositor's accounts in order for banks to remain solvent..."[28]

"Banks move to negative interest rates on cash deposits - could this lead to a cashless/digital currency?"

---

[28] Mark Nestmann, "It's Official: The Worldwide Bail-ins Are Coming," *Nestmann* December 23, 2014, http://www.nestmann.com/its-official-the-worldwide-bail-ins-are-coming#.VgV-Q_lViko

"Central Banks are already attempting to dump physical cash..."[29]

Young people today are increasingly concerned over their loss of privacy, and certainly the Patriot Act has been pivotal to the loss of privacy. It behooves every American citizen to consider a cashless society where hackers, both domestic and state-sponsored from Russia and China, can gain access to your accounts and wipe out your savings. The only solution the government will offer you for protection of your digital bank accounts will be biometrics or an electronic implant. Your physical body will become your only protection against theft. Once physical cash goes away, all anonymity is gone; the banking system will control all of your financial transactions, and NSA will collect and track all other electronic data.

"Bank notes, as an alternate storehouse of value, are a constraint on central bank's power. We view this constraint as undesirable," Citigroup Global Chief Economist Willem Buiter and a colleague,

---

[29] Peter Coy, "The Death of Cash: Could Negative Interest Rates Create an Existential Crisis for Money Itself?, *Bloomberg* April 23, 2015, http://www.bloomberg.com/news/articles/2015-04-23/negative-interest-rates-may-spark-existential-crisis-for-cash.

economist Ebrahim Rahbari, wrote in an April 8, 2015, research piece. They laid out three ways that central banks could foil cash hoarders: One, abolish paper money. Two, tax paper money. Three, sever the link between paper money and central bank reserves.[30]

"Centralization of credit in the hands of the state, by means of a national bank with state capital and an exclusive monopoly."

—Ten Planks of the Communist Manifesto—Karl Marx

"Let me issue and control a nation's money and I care not who writes the laws."

—Mayer Amschel Rothschild (1744-1812), founder of the House of Rothschild

With the world economic crisis on the horizon, and most, if not all, of the G-20 countries facing insolvency, the first option of the central banks will be the "bail-in" scenario where the banks will confiscate the accounts of depositors, and then dole out money on a limited basis for you to buy food and fuel.

---

[30] http://www.bloomberg.com/news/articles/2015-04-23/negative-interest-rates-may-spark-existential-crisis-for-cash.

Inevitably, when this fails, world financial systems will quickly transition to digital money. With the vulnerability of the electronic systems, they will move to biometrics or electronic implants to prevent anyone but account holders from making unauthorized withdrawals. At that point the government will have complete control of the population.

Many in the United States do not realize that the Federal Reserve is a private banking cartel established in 1913. Bankers, communists, and the global elite understand that control of a nation is exercised through centralized banking.

As G. Edward Griffin points out in *The Creature from Jekyll Island*, the Federal Reserve was created to stabilize our economy:

> *Since its inception, it has presided over the crashes of 1921 and 1929; the Great Depression of '29 to '39; recessions in '53, '57, '69, '75, and '81; a stock market "Black Monday" in '87; and a 1000% inflation which has destroyed 90% of the dollar's purchasing power. Let us be more specific on that last point. By 1990, an annual income of $10,000*

was required to buy what took only $1,000 in 1914.[31]

The following consumer price index chart shows how inflation has grown in the United States since the creation of the Federal Reserve. Inflation is commonly referred to as the "hidden tax." Inflation happens when the government prints currency out of nothing. The more money they print, the more your dollars are devalued, which results in the higher cost of goods and services.

Figure 1. Consumer Price Index, United States, 1775-2012
(level, 1775=1)

Sources: Bureau of Labor Statistics, Historical Statistics of the United States, and Reinhart and Rogoff (2009).[32]

---

[31] G.Edward Griffin, *The Creature from Jekyll Island*, (Westlake Village CA: American Media, 2010), 20.
[32] Sam Ro, "Chart: Inflation Since 1775 And How It Took Off in 1933," *Business Insider* Jan.6,2013, http://www.businessinsider.com/chart-inflation-since-1775 2013-1

Shortly after the creation of the central bank, the Federal Reserve, President Franklin D. Roosevelt gave the banking cartel another powerful tool for confiscating the personal property and wealth of American citizens. In 1933, he set the price of an ounce of gold at $20.60. In 1934, the government raised the price of one ounce of gold to $35, where it remained until 1971 when President Nixon took the United States completely off the gold standard.

The currency of the United States became full-fledged fiat currency in 1971, meaning it had no redeemable value. Its value was established by government decree and not tied to or convertible to gold or silver. The banking cartel now had the ability to print money at will. The more they print, the less value of the dollar in your pocket. In the following chart you will see the hockey stick of national debt, and how it relates to the hockey stick graph of inflation.

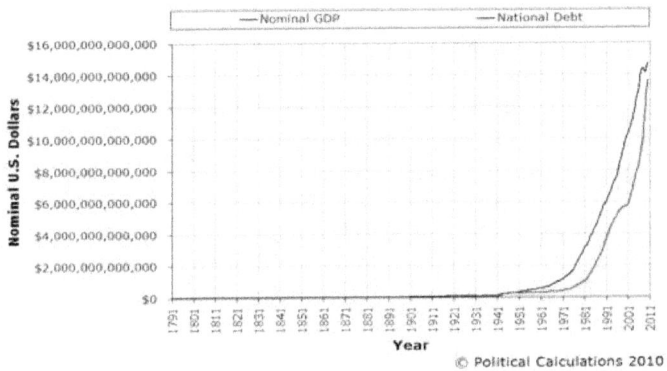

U.S. Annual GDP and National Debt, 1791-2010

— Nominal GDP   — National Debt

© Political Calculations 2010

33

In simple terms, the Federal Reserve was created to give the largest banks control of the money supply so those big banks would never lose, no matter how unethical their business practices were. The bigger the risky loan they make, the more profit they will see from the interest they earn on the loan. In simplistic terms, big banks make risky loans, even when they logically know the borrower will never be able to repay the debt. They collect interest until the borrower cannot repay, and then they either make another loan and collect even more interest, or reschedule the loan to ensure they continue to collect interest.

---

[33] Ironman, "Visualizing the U.S. National Debt: 1791-2010," *Political Calculations* December 14, 2010, http://politicalcalculations.blogspot.com/2010/12/visualizing-us-national-debt-1791-2010.html#.Vf4OpEuVygM

Banks never want the borrower to default, but when they do, Congress and the Federal Reserve come to the bank's rescue.

When the time comes that the borrower's debt is too large and the borrower is ready to default, the banks simply go to Congress and present the case that corporation X is "too big to fail." If the government does not assume responsibility for debt repayment, there will be a devastating impact on the entire U.S. or international financial system. Remember, the Federal Reserve has no reserve, so they print government debt by issuing credit money, or in other words, print money with only the good will of the American taxpayer to pay the debt. The bank that made the bad loan suffers no loss; indeed, they profit. They earned interest on bad loans and the government secures the principle through the taxpayers. It's a huge win for the banks— they continue to grow their wealth while the American citizen picks up the debt.

Without representation, the taxpayer is held accountable each and every time the Federal Reserve releases new money to pay off bad loans made by banks. With every release of fiat money by the Federal Reserve, the taxpayer ends up paying more for every purchase because his dollar has been diluted by the influx of newly-printed money that is not backed by any redeemable value. That is the "hidden tax" known as inflation.

In *The Creature from Jekyll Island*, Griffin details the multiple times "too big to fail" has been used to the benefit of large banks and their primary stockholders. Griffin provides insight into the government bailout of investment banking during 2008:

Merrill Lynch: A Gift to Bank of America

In the fall of 2008, the giant brokerage house, Merrill Lynch, was out of money and on the verge of closing its doors. Bank of America agreed to buy the ailing firm for $50 billion, a strange offer considering that the Bank, itself, was in trouble and recently received $25 billion in bailout. When the staggering fourth-quarter losses of Merrill Lynch were finally known, the Bank decided to back out of the deal. But this was not to be allowed. According to the sworn testimony of Ken Lewis, Bank of America's CEO, Treasury Secretary, Hank Paulson, threatened to remove the bank's board of directors and its management *if they didn't acquire Merrill as agreed. This threat was made at the request of Ben Bernanke, Chairman of the Federal Reserve. When Lewis asked if the government would cover the banks inevitable losses, Paulson said, 'yes,' but was not willing to put it in writing, because a written commitment, he said, 'would be a disclosable event, and we do not want a disclosable event.'*

On December 30th, the bank's board dutifully approved the merger. Two weeks later, the Treasury delivered to the Bank of America an additional $20 billion plus a $118 billion guarantee to pick up further losses from Merrill's assets. All of that was placed on the backs of the American people.

An Icon for Conflict of Interest

Henry Paulson (Chairman of the Federal Reserve) was the epitome of the fusion between the banking cartel and government. As former CEO of Goldman Sachs, he was instrumental in using the power of his office to destroy three of his old rivals. He arranged the sale of Bear Sterns to JP Morgan Chase, allowed Lehman Brothers to collapse, and forced the absorption of Merrill Lynch by the Bank of America, all the while providing a generous bailout for his alma mater, Goldman Sachs. This left only Goldman and Morgan as major investment banks.[34]

Griffin provides a comprehensive study on the Federal Reserve in *The Creature from Jekyll Island*. If it were required reading in our national public school system, we would see the death of the creature in our lifetime.

Ideally, we would like to see the end of the Federal Reserve. Congressman Ron Paul wrote a book in 2009: *End The Fed*. Others have called for an audit of the Federal Reserve. Neither is likely to occur in our current political culture. In 1984, Jack Kemp authored a bill to return to the Gold Standard—it was defeated. See the bill below:

---

[34] Griffin, *The Creature from Jekyll Island*, 58, 59.

Gold Standard Act of 1984 —Requires the Secretary of the Treasury, by one year after enactment of this Act, to establish a permanent definition of the dollar, expressed as a fixed weight of gold, nine-tenths fine.

Declares that the dollar so defined shall be the standard and unit of value of the United States. Permits any person, after such time, to redeem for gold at any Federal Reserve bank any currency or coin of the United States or any demand note or demand liability of a Federal Reserve bank. Requires the Secretary to mint gold coins in such weights, denominations, and forms as will best serve the maintenance of gold payments and the needs of commerce.

Makes such gold coins legal tender for all debts, public charges, taxes, and dues.

Permits the exchange of gold bullion for gold coins, which contain an equal weight of fine gold minus a charge that shall not exceed mint costs and related expenses.

Requires the Secretary and the Board of Governors of the Federal Reserve System to prescribe rules and regulations to carry out this Act. Repeals restrictions on gold payments and gold ownership.

If the Gold Standard is not re-established, it is certain that we will see the end of physical currency. It will be replaced by digital currency, and you will lose all privacy and, with that, all freedom. Digital currency will further empower the central banking system of the Federal Reserve and its crony banking cartel members to confiscate the property of every American citizen. The government will control your bank accounts and every expenditure you make. You will become a complete ward of the state. You are the only one standing between freedom and tyranny. You need to fully familiarize yourself with our banking system, educate anyone who will listen, and stand with those who want to restore soundness to our banking system. Above all else, you need to oppose the removal of physical currency if you want to save our last trace of freedom.

Leadership

"But the leaders of His people trampled prisoners underfoot.
They deprived people of their God-given rights in defiance
of the Most High. They perverted justice in the courts. Do
they think the Lord didn't see it?"
—Lamentations 3:34

Leadership is not defined by power or position. It is responsibility, authority, and accountability. Honorable leadership is always a path to success and not necessarily wealth, fame, or power. It will produce teamwork, creativity, initiative, encouragement, and excellence. It is success that is shared by everyone on the team. It is success that can only be accomplished through courage, morality, and integrity.

Leadership sets standards of excellence, produces shared success, and accomplishes the mission through the willing and motivated participation of people. Leadership can be measured by its positive impact on the lives of those who follow. Leadership is seen in teamwork singularly focused on common goals, ethical standards, and mission accomplishment. When leaders put people first, success always follows.

Political corruption, moral decay, high taxes, inflation, unemployment, entertainment for the masses, entanglement in foreign wars, and unrestricted immigration destroyed Rome long before its fall to Germanic tribes in 476 A.D. After five hundred years, arguably one of the most powerful empires the world has known, Rome, was destroyed from within. Politicians drained the treasury to appease the population with free bread and entertainment in order to remain in power. Corruption and life without moral restraint made a once strong and proud people weak and dependent, nothing more than sheep for slaughter.

Can a people remain free without moral, principled leadership? History is a grim reminder of the decline of nations when leadership fails to remain courageous, honorable, and committed to truth. We live in an emasculated society where truth has become a casualty in the war of political correctness and self-indulgence. When someone does speak the truth they are labeled as a bigot, racist, or as someone having some type of phobia. Truth has become the victim. Our nation has become one where what was right is now wrong—a place where people call what is evil, good; and what is good, evil.

The laws of nature determine that leadership will always occur; leadership vacuums do not exist anywhere in nature. Leadership takes many forms, from tribal societies to complex modern governments, but there will always be some form of leadership. Even on the playground, you will see leadership among children—some child is out there determining what the rest are doing. You might be born with charisma, but leadership and charisma are not synonymous. Leadership skills can only be learned, exercised, and perfected. The question remains and can only be answered by you: What role will you play?

Our country is in dire need of honorable, principled leaders in all walks of life, and it is time for you to step up to the challenge. No nation in history has survived leadership that was immoral and unethical. Unfortunately, we have those in abundance in our country. Leaders in all walks of life need to step up within their realm of responsibility and authority to restore our wayward nation and turn around what today seems like a hopeless situation.

Leaders are not born—they are created. Whether you lead one or many, you can daily improve your skills to become a better leader. The following are a few lessons in leadership that I learned in the Marine Corps which can be used by you to restore our nation.

1. *"But he who is greatest among you shall be your servant."* —Matthew 23:11

During Boot Camp and Officer Candidate School, the Marine Corps teaches that leaders always eat last. It has practical application designed to ensure that the food is of the same quality and quantity at the end of the line as it is at the beginning. This is not the typical model you see in the world today. Go to any gathering, conference, or banquet and observe who eats first. It inevitably will be the head table, the honored guests, the VIPs who are first to partake. When the leader eats last, it ripples down the chain of command ending with the least being served first. What a difference it would make in our world if leaders in industry, business, and government focused first on the needs of others. This type of leadership models the ideal that with rank comes responsibility, before privilege. It puts greed, power, and personal desire in the proper position—at the end of the line.

Leadership is not position; it does not demand respect or accommodation. It is not weak, submissive or cowardly. It is indifferent to public applause and popular culture. This model of sacrifice is decidedly different from what is witnessed in contemporary America. Who stands at the front of your line— your subordinates or the privileged, powerful, wealthy, popular people? Who is the least among you and where do they stand?

2. *"Try not to become a man of success, but rather try to become a man of value."* —Albert Einstein

If you asked most people to define success, they would generally describe it as the accumulation of wealth, fame, prominent position of power, or all three. All three can be achieved through a variety of paths, and all three have the potential of being powerful corruptors of mankind. They are not inherently bad—it depends on the motivation of the person who acquires them, the paths people take to achieve them, and what they do with them once they acquire them.

We all know people who have acquired wealth, fame, and power through immoral and unethical means, leaving a wake of destruction in their path through fear, exploitation, and abuse. The shortest path to the top is usually accomplished on the backs of others. This kind of "success" is always acquired at the expense of other people and cannot be confused with leadership; simply defined, it is manipulation.

3. *"Leaders don't create followers, they create more leaders."*

—Tom Peters

The ultimate goal of any good leader is to produce better leaders. The practical reasons for developing leaders in your organization is to "spread load" the leadership responsibilities throughout the organization. By sharing responsibility, authority, and accountability at appropriate levels throughout an organization, you remove bottlenecks in the decision-making process and open floodgates of efficiency. Every effective subordinate leader you produce shares the burden of leadership by finding solutions and eliminating problems before they have an opportunity to bog down the chain of command.

Developing leaders is not for the faint-hearted, risk-adverse, or zero-defect leaders. It requires you to logically evaluate your workload and determine which requirements you can and should delegate to someone else. It requires that you evaluate who best can fulfill that requirement and then properly train them to accomplish the task. The very nature of leadership development demands intuition and patience.

4. *"Don't be a Caesar—drunk with power and self-importance: it happens all too easily. Keep yourself simple, good, pure, sincere, natural, just, god-fearing, kind,*

affectionate, and devoted to your duty... Fear God; serve mankind. Life is short; the only good fruit to be harvested in this earthly realm requires a pious disposition and charitable behavior."[35] —Marcus Aurelius

As Second Lieutenants, we were taught everything by the book and then tested or inspected on what we had learned. We were taught that you could only expect the results you want to achieve by the things that you inspect—expect what you inspect. I remember having every uniform we owned inspected, tailored, and re-inspected until it was perfect. Our minds were immersed with every uniform regulation of the Corps. The reason was simple: As a platoon commander you would be required to perform uniform inspections on your platoon. The theory was that while you had one set of eyes to inspect 39, there were 39 sets of eyes inspecting you. It was a critical lesson that everyone learned but many forgot—and it had nothing to do with uniforms.

Leaders who think that subordinates are not watching them all the time are sadly mistaken. Every leader is going to make mistakes, so do not concern yourself with trying to hide them; your mistakes are usually known and broadcast faster than

---

[35] Aurelius, *The Emperor's Handbook*, 70.

a tsunami warning. Mistakes are inevitable. Willful violations of standards, moral infractions, and ethical shortcomings are not, and no matter what you think, they are being registered, recorded, and documented by your subordinates. Of note, your personal honor and integrity will also do more to set the standards than your words.

5. *"Rebellion to tyrants is obedience to God."* —Thomas Jefferson

SgtMaj Roberts, my first battalion SgtMaj, used to say, *"Don't mistake my good manners for weakness."* If you have to tell people you are the boss and in control, then you are not at all. Everyone knows who the boss is by virtue of position. You maintain control by never losing control of yourself. If you have lost control, you have a serious problem; your subordinates do not respect you. Your position is not in question—your ability and credibility are.

The surest way to start a rebellion in your organization is to become a tyrant. They will bow to the wishes of the ill-mannered, irreverent, power-of-the-position only out of fear, not respect. You might never face open rebellion, but you will find people slow-rolling requirements, mediocre performance, and low morale.

No amount of cussing, yelling, or threatening will change the lazy, incompetent person, or make people care who couldn't care less. Out-of-control leadership is just that—out of control, nothing more—and it will never motivate a workforce to excel.

Good manners will never categorize you as a weak, ineffective leader. Well-thought-out responses to problems, failure, and difficult people, with the appropriate level of attention, will gain respect and challenge the hardest cases, whereas loss of control will breed contempt with both good and bad subordinates.

6. *"Integrity is the antithesis of compromise and the sworn enemy of comfort. It bases its decisions not on how much discomfort we might be able to avoid, but on how much we need to avoid the compromise of comfort."* —Craig D. Lounsbrough

The road to hell is paved with compromise. We have watched the destruction of our laws, sovereignty, and morals through compromise. Compromise has become the cultural lexicon for progressive thought and equitable treatment. However, if you look up the definition of compromise in the dictionary it is defined as: *"agree by conceding, lessen the value* of somebody or something, and expose somebody or something to danger."

All leaders make mistakes, but decisions to compromise principle always lead to the destruction of someone or something. Compromise is the slow erosion of your leadership foundation one little brick at a time. Eventually, you will find that you have no foundation left to stand on, and you have sacrificed your moral authority to be an effective leader. Compromise only survives in an environment of moral cowardice. The compromise of principle might earn friends, but it will never earn respect. Even the most unprincipled of people want to be led by principled and just leaders.

7. The First Law of Thermodynamics: "When the heat is on someone else it's not on you." —Unknown

Leaders are insulators while managers are conductors. Everyone has worked for someone who can't take the heat and immediately passes the pain they feel from the boss to every subordinate in close proximity. Those people are managers. They manage the pain they feel by passing it on to someone else. Mistakes are never an option; managers function only in a zero defect world. When mistakes happen, managers are most comfortable spreading the pain and always the blame; they seem

151

to believe it dissipates the heat that is directed to them. Unfortunately, they seldom pass on any praise they might have received from the success brought on by their subordinates.

Overreaction is the key characteristic of a manager. They overreact to any criticism or any mistake they feel will negatively reflect on them or their career. For instance, if one subordinate screws something up, they mandate a new regulation that punishes everyone. Instead of focusing on the perpetrator they make every subordinate feel the pain. If someone abuses a privilege or authority they take that privilege or authority from everyone. They attempt to control or regulate every action of their subordinates in order to protect their own career. These managers eventually squelch all creativity and initiative in an organization by restricting the abilities of the many for the indiscretion of the few. If you want to crush morale, punish innocent people for the mistakes of others.

Leaders, however, are insulators. They never let their subordinates feel the pain they experience. They take the mantle of leadership and responsibility seriously and protect subordinates from unwarranted and extreme abuse that sometimes flows from the top. They never pull back authority and responsibility from those who have earned or deserve those privileges.

8. *"Stop dithering around. In every confrontation, render what is just; from every impression, extract what is true."*[36]
—Marcus Aurelius

Leaders are responsible for the process, not every outcome. Although the leader's job is to influence outcomes, only dictators try to control every outcome. Subordinates want enough direction to understand what you expect, but lose all job satisfaction when you micro-manage their every step. People thrive when challenged; they and their spirit wither when their every step is controlled. If you want to destroy motivation, creativity, and initiative, you can effectively do so by deciding every step of the process.

People also thrive in disciplined environments where rules are justly and universally enforced. As a leader you will set the right and left boundaries of acceptable behavior. You will set those boundaries by the written rules of your organization and by the example you set. Remember, you are always being watched and evaluated. Should you ignore boundary violations of

---

[36] Aurelius, *The Emperor's Handbook*, 46.

subordinates, you will be labeled as weak; should you willingly violate rules, you will be considered a hypocrite and lose your moral authority.

Discipline does not mean every violation is treated the same; there are always variables that require both justice and mercy. Discipline means that you always address violations. Situations determine the severity of the discipline; sometimes issues are addressed with a counseling, sometimes much more, but as a leader you always address infractions. You are responsible for the integrity of the organization.

9. "Surround yourself with good people and delegate."
—Ronald Reagan

Do competent people scare you? Are you afraid of having people work for you who are smarter, more articulate, better looking, and all around more capable than you? Unfortunately, capable and competent subordinates intimidate far too many people in leadership positions. They make it their mission in life to keep highly capable subordinates from rising above them.

I always spent my time trying to find people who were better than me. I was secure in my position and familiar enough with my own shortcomings to know that the unit would only get better with people who could make up for my shortcomings. Ultimately, I always benefited from surrounding myself with good people.

You seldom have the opportunity to build the ideal team to support your vision, but when you do, get the best and brightest. Shelve your ego and the perception that as the boss you have to be the best or smartest, and you will never be disappointed in the results your people produce. Leaders guide, direct, mentor, and encourage subordinates to accomplish the mission. When it becomes all about you and your ego rather than the mission, you stop being a leader and become a self-serving tyrant.

10. *"The beauty of empowering others is that your own power is not diminished in the process."* — Barbara Colorose

I learned over the years that most people want to know where the goal line is, and what the right and left boundaries are. They want to use the whole field to accomplish the mission and not be told how to run every play. Of equal importance, they want to know what is out of bounds, and they expect leaders to hold them accountable when they step out of bounds. If you want to accomplish more, then give others room to operate, guide them toward the goal line, and do not direct every step.

I assumed battalion command with what I perceived as worthwhile ideas on how to better train and equip the Marines and Sailors of the Battalion for an upcoming combat deployment. As clearly as I could, I lay out what I thought was a clear plan. However, with each weekly meeting, there seemed to be more questions and less progress toward the goal.

I was continually bombarded by detailed questions on how I wanted things done. When the process started, I figured I had a year to get the command prepared for a future deployment, but that all suddenly changed when we were left with two months of preparation time; it seemed like we still had not left the starting blocks. I called the leadership of the battalion to a meeting. I held up my hand and said, "*You are all empowered to make decisions to move us forward*" and began ticking off my fingers with the questions they needed to ask themselves with their newfound authority.

1. Is it good for the Marine Corps?
2. Is it good for the mission?
3. Is it good for the Marines and Sailors?
4. Is it legal?

5. Most important of all, is it ethical?

I told them if they could answer those questions affirmatively they did not need to delay the process by asking me for detailed guidance.

11. "*One of the very worst uses of time is to do something very well that need not to be done at all.*" —Brian Tracy

College, business management, military, and civilian leadership classes all teach that leaders and managers will spend 90 percent of their time with 10 percent of the people—the 10 percent prone to cause trouble. This 90 percent rule was repeatedly emphasized and utilized in every command. Everyone I knew would simply shrug their shoulders and acquiesce to the 90 percent rule. I followed suit through three command tours until I realized it did not have to be that way.

The day I took over as a battalion commander, I learned that I had a backlog of legal challenges brought on by a few bad actors. We spent months going through the grind of spending too much time on the "wrong" people. Fortunately, our battalion was called on a short notice deployment to Iraq. That was a game changer; there was no time left for working deals, rehabilitation, or entertaining the complaints of the troublemakers. We had training requirements to meet: dental and medical readiness, weapons qualification, equipment readiness, logistics, and administration to accomplish in about one-fifth of the normal time.

I called the staff NCOs and officers together and told them we were going to focus on the team. We no longer had the luxury of devoting time with the non-team players. Realistically, non-team players are self-absorbed with either their own agenda or puffed up with their own self-importance. I made the decision that leadership would spend 90 percent of our time with 90 percent of the people. We instituted a process that did not allow the troublemakers the opportunity to monopolize leadership time.

The 10 percent will always be the 10 percent. Think about how many individuals you have actually rehabilitated, and do not waste your time trying to change people. Address issues as necessary and move on. You will be amazed at the results when you start spending 90 percent of your time with 90 percent of your people.

This is by no means a comprehensive list of leadership principles and traits, but it will get you started. Leadership, like every profession, requires daily study and application for improvement and excellence. If you have already chosen to be a leader, I sincerely congratulate you; if you are new to the principles outlined, welcome. Know this: Our country needs your leadership.

Conclusion

Be like a rocky promontory against which the
restless surf continually pounds; it stands fast
while the churning sea is lulled to sleep at its
feet. I hear you say, 'How unlucky that this
should happen to me!' Not at all! Say instead,
'How lucky that I am not broken by what has
happened and am not afraid of what is about
to happen. The same blow might have struck
anyone, but not many would have absorbed it
without capitulation or complaint.'

After all, why do we speak of good luck and
bad luck anyway? Would you call something
that is not contrary to a man's nature a piece
of bad luck? And can something be contrary
to a man's nature that nature wills? Well, you
know perfectly well what nature wills. Do the

waves that crash upon you prevent you in any way from being just, forgiving, moderate, discerning, truthful, loyal, free-spirited, and in possession of all the other noble qualities that nature wills for man's well-being? The next time you are tempted to complain of your bad luck, remember to apply this maxim: 'Bad luck borne nobly is good luck.' [37]

—Marcus Aurelius

We live in some of the most exciting, and at the same time challenging, times our nation has ever known. Unlike many, I am not pessimistic about our future. The person who will restore our nation is you. You are the George Washington, Thomas Jefferson, or Benjamin Franklin of today. Stop looking to the right, left, or behind you; focus on the task before you. When you stand, you will stiffen the spine of the person standing next to you and behind you.

A strong, vital relationship with God is essential as you commit your unique capabilities to the restoration tasks ahead for our families, churches, schools, and government. Imagine 100,000,000 others just like you committing themselves to the

---

[37] Aurelius, *The Emperor's Handbook*, 51.

restoration of our country. There are many organizations you can join that have been fighting the good fight to restore our nation. While many work toward worthy causes, they will fail when they do not look to the root of the causes that are destroying our nation—primarily, the erosion of morality and faith in God in our society. Without God, you are left with situational morality; without God you have no religion. Without a belief in ultimate accountability, man is left with what he can get away with in this world.

We are in a war for our very survival. Though the beacon of freedom burns dimly, it has not been extinguished. The United States, like every great nation in history, is being destroyed from within. Immorality, welfare, entertainment, and unconstrained immigration destroyed the Roman Empire, and it will destroy the United States if left unchecked. We need to restore the Constitution. There are those who say the Constitution is outdated and cannot function in a technological society. Their assumptions are utterly false. The Constitution, as written, was impartial and unaffected by technology; it was written to restrain the passions of men who desire to enslave and control other men. Our Constitution was written not to protect the majority, but the rights of the smallest minority—the individual—and that individual is you.

In this war for our nation we need to identify the enemy. The enemies are two private organizations that have taken control of our nation. Although they appear to be different, they have achieved singularity in purpose: The destruction of the one document, our Constitution, which stands between freedom and slavery. You can choose to swear your allegiance to the Democrat party or the Republican party, or you can choose to swear allegiance to <u>our country</u>.

The power of these singular-in-purpose, private organizations is ignorance. As a people we are not well schooled on our Constitution; therefore, we are unaware of our rights. We have empowered this new aristocracy to take away our rights and dole out privilege and favor to their faithful supporters. Truth and knowledge of the Constitution in the hands of the population empowers each and every one of us to wage a successful war against those who want to enslave the citizenry of the United States. Should you fail to learn and assert your rights, you will be left to beg crumbs from the table of your unjust rulers. Nobody knows how much time we have, but it is certain that the time is short. It is critical to employ your time in striving to restore our country and return to a Constitutional government. The power brokers will never cede power back to the people. This is not a single battle that can be won and forgotten—it is a continuous war to ensure that the power of our nation resides with the people.

> *"Be a boxer, not a gladiator, in the way you act on your principles. The gladiator takes up his sword only to put it down again, but the boxer is never without his fist and has only to clench it."* [38]
>
> —Marcus Aurelius

You can no longer wait for someone else. If you do not stand today, your country will certainly be gone tomorrow. It is time for you to lead—either you run for office or you find capable, honest men and women who fear God and hate bribes. Nominate and support those brave individuals. You will achieve victory if you speak the truth, love God, and love your neighbor.

> *"He has shown you, O man, what is good; and what does the Lord require of you but to do justly, to love mercy, and to walk humbly with your God."*
>
> —Micah 6:3

---

[38] Aurelius, *The Emperor's Handbook*, 139.